I PLACE
MY HANDS
IN HIS

I PLACE MY HANDS IN HIS

Forty Days of Devotions

Dr. Selene Maya Author

ARCHWAY
PUBLISHING

Archway Publishing books may be ordered through booksellers or by contacting:

Archway Publishing
1663 Liberty Drive
Bloomington, IN 47403
www.archwaypublishing.com
1 (888) 242-5904

Because of the dynamic nature of the Internet, any web addresses or links contained in this book may have changed since publication and may no longer be valid. The views expressed in this work are solely those of the author and do not necessarily reflect the views of the publisher, and the publisher hereby disclaims any responsibility for them.

Any people depicted in stock imagery provided by Getty Images are models, and such images are being used for illustrative purposes only. Certain stock imagery © Getty Images.

Scriptures taken from the Holy Bible, New International Version®, NIV®. Copyright © 1973, 1978, 1984, 2011 by Biblica, Inc.™ Used by permission of Zondervan. All rights reserved worldwide. www.zondervan. com The "NIV" and "New International Version" are trademarks registered in the United States Patent and Trademark Office by Biblica, Inc.™

ISBN: 978-1-4808-5979-1 (sc)
ISBN: 978-1-4808-5977-7 (hc)
ISBN: 978-1-4808-5978-4 (e)

Library of Congress Control Number: 2018903367

Print information available on the last page.

Archway Publishing rev. date: 04/24/2018

To my darlings: my beloved children Andrew, Ryan, and yes, my very own flower, Mala. I am humbled and grateful that God saw fit to bless me with three amazing angels. Thank you for the gift of being your mother. You will forever be my roses.

CONTENTS

INTRODUCTION

My message to you is that if you feel that the world has abandoned you and you have abandoned yourself, God has not! Joel 2:25 (NIV) says, "'I will repay you for the years the locusts have eaten— the great locust and the young locust, the other locusts and the locust swarm— my great army that I sent among you." God will use everything for His glory. The good, bad and the ugly, it's all preordained to build you into a giant slayer. So whatever situations you are facing, find the strength to rise up! Remember that He is working it all out for your growth and empowerment. Even what seems to be the smallest things, do not give up; your breakthrough is on the cusp! Here is my story.

After completing my book, *Silent Cry Loud Echo: God Heard Me*, a project I had worked on for a few years, I expected the feeling of accomplishment and the bliss of completion to hold me in good stead and buoy my spirits. I thought that by sharing my personal story, the stark truths, and detailing my emotions and path of personal growth, it would help me release all the pain I had buried deep within.

Much to my surprise and disappointment, I was left feeling the polar opposite: uncentered, off-balanced, and depressed. I knew that I was being compelled to speak—to be transparent in hopes that my honest connection with you would propel you into your own path way of discovering your peaceful place and settling into contentment with you and God. And that you would trust Him wholeheartedly, for He knows the plan He has for you.

As I thought of my journey and recorded my story onto paper, many emotions resurfaced; the hurt of the traumatic years that I had tried to suppress and keep deeply buried and forgotten was ever so real. I began to grieve for that young girl who had endured years of turmoil; I wanted to go back in time and protect her. While I regurgitated the details of my story, teardrops fell on my keyboard as I recounted and relived both the pain from my past and the feelings of gratitude that God had set me free from the trauma of rape, abandonment, and years of abuse.

Dear reader, don't get me wrong. I'm grateful for all that I've gone through, but the memories of digging deep within my past brought up things that I had consciously suppressed. This, in turn, affected me more physically than I could have imagined, which caused me to become mentally drained and emotionally exhausted. I realized I had simply been surviving, and the pain of confrontation is not as easy but necessary.

So many of us live from day to day, simply waiting and wondering why we are still alive. You might have asked God to take your life because the pain of living was simply too much, but from my experience, God will *not* take you before your time is up. So for this reason, I pray that you will turn your attention to living and accompanying God's promise for you. God has a plan for our lives, and we must believe this. Living in such mental turmoil affects all aspects of our lives. I lived in agony, and the face I showed the world was quite different from the one I took to bed at nights. I tossed and turned with little sleep.

As a result, I gained an unhealthy amount of weight. This is a powerful example of how stress can be a deadly contributor and a detriment to your health. I remember being told not to overeat when upset because when the body is under stress, it is not able to process food properly, and food is harder to digest in this condition. Nevertheless, in spite of knowing these facts, food was my drug of choice!

So for those of us who use food or any other form of drugs as a reliever of stress, consider the health consequences. Let's make a decision to know our body and honor this beautiful and amazing gift God has given us. My beloved, it is my sincerest desire for you to be well and to get professional help. I love you as my brothers and sisters in Christ. We are all connected in the spirit.

This reminds me of when I was attending a conference for Doctors of Natural Medicine a while ago. I learned that when you are ill, you should go on a liquid fast. I believe this process will give the body a chance to rest and heal. After all, isn't that what the animals instinctively do? They must know something we don't. Jesus wants us to love ourselves as He loves us.

In spite of the detrimental side effects that worrying, stress, and improper diet can cause, I realized writing the first book was truly an adventure on all counts. Although unsettling emotions were churned up, there was a sense of satisfaction that God and I had completed our goal in spite of the hurdles I had encountered. It was truly a labor of love for me and was done in a spirit to benefit God's people. I wanted people to realize the devastating effects of domestic violence, self-neglect, improper nutrition, and depression, and the trauma they cause to you and everyone involved. You have hurt long enough. It's your turn to heal!

So on the journey in birthing my first book, I encountered roadblocks and obstacles, and I overcame many hurdles to get my work completed. However, hard work and perseverance are the keys to accomplishing anything.

Not surprisingly, I was lost at sea when it came to knowing the sequencing of steps and the process of turning my life experiences into a narrative to share with others. Although I had written my story line to reflect the present state of my heart, it seemed that for every step forward, I was given misguided information and was even misled in so many ways. None of these were able to affect me as much as one particular individual.

I came across a person who proclaimed to be anointed and was there to facilitate my efforts. At first I was reluctant. Nevertheless, I decided to let my guard down and be vulnerable.

Unfortunately, I was taken in by this person. I had been hoping for positive direction and reinforcing guidance, and I had naively put my faith and trust in this person's "good intentions." Little did I know that my faith was woefully misplaced. The misdirected faith and trust nearly derailed years of work. In spite of it all I kept my laser-beam drive and focus.

Loyalty, responsibility, and trust are personal traits that I hold in high regard. When these feelings are properly placed, they can manifest themselves in ways that are most beneficial and rewarding. In retrospect, they can also be like a double-edged sword, wounding us severely when they are not reciprocated. With this being said, as part of being well, we must be aware of who we chose to let close to us. Be careful who you allow to mentor you. Trust God for guidance at all times and never be quick to make important decisions.

As Christians, we are called to take on the personality of God. The world is particularly harsh, but assumption of this personality calls us to conduct ourselves accordingly.

So to those who have been wounded by a person in leadership, I pray that God may heal your damaged soul. I pray that you find the strength to forgive, move forward, and place your pain under the blood of Jesus. This journey of triumph is definitely for us!

In spite of all the setbacks, and the consequences of my misguided actions, I felt the need to forgive, redouble my efforts, and get back on the right track.

I instinctively feel my life's purpose, and I knew that I needed to continue to walk in that calling, regardless of the magnitude of the setback. I knew that the only way to move beyond my experiences was to start all over again. I had much too much to do, and if I were ever to finish my project, I could make no other choice. Move forward and do not look back!

I was determined to trust God in the process; after all, He hadn't failed me yet, and He always made a way for me when it seemed impossible to continue.

Although forgiving and opting to not take legal action should have settled my spirit and propelled me forward, the ordeal only served to make me feel more physically beaten down than I had felt before.

I had been through many daunting trials and tribulations before, but God had never allowed them to break me. I was determined to not allow myself to fall any further into despair. It was then that I reached out for a divine handhold.

Wayne Dyer once said, "With everything that has happened to you, you can either feel sorry for yourself, or treat what has happened as a gift. Everything is either an opportunity to grow, or an obstacle to keep you from growing. You get to choose."

As I have done in the past, I sought my answers from God. Although I had always felt His presence in my life, this time I really needed to hear His voice to know His direction, purpose, and plan for me.

It was as an unsated hunger in me and a deep internal void that I needed to fill. I began fasting and praying as I continued to seek God's face for healing and His wisdom for guidance and perspective.

After some period of time, I received the word from Him that I had been so desperately seeking. My friends, no matter who you are and where you are with Christ, growth requires drawing nearer to God and allowing Him to speak to your hearts, changing us from the inside out. We must listen to His instructions for guidance in all aspects of our lives.

The revelation from God was made clear when I heard God say, "Forty days!"

He told me He would heal me by taking me on a forty-day journey and that the fruits and insights of my journey were to be shared with His people. It would be a journey of grounding for the soul, body, mind, and spirit. Furthermore, in order to return me to my true and former self, it would include a complementary alignment of diet, exercise, and nutritional supplements.

The appearance of the number forty in His revelation puzzled me at first. I began to diligently research the scriptures to find what, if any, significance there was to that particular number.

Much to my surprise, I found that this number was strategically mentioned in the Bible almost one hundred fifty times.

I further learned that when viewed in terms of time, the number forty denotes a period of testing, trials, and probation. How this resonated with my current predicament!

In Exodus 34:27–28 (NIV), Moses fasted upon the mountaintop for forty days and nights, seeking the presence of God, and searching for divine direction. "Then the Lord said to Moses, 'Write down these words, for in accordance with these words I have made a covenant with you and with Israel.' Moses was there with the Lord forty days and forty nights without eating bread or drinking water. And he wrote on the tablets the words of the covenant—the Ten Commandments."

Our life can and will be encased in chaos without God's divine direction. As we embark on this forty-day journey, I invite and encourage you to place your hands in His and walk with me into the glory of God's higher calling and anointing for your life.

Leave your life print of who you were created to be. We only have one go around at life, make it impactful.

To my readers and all the nations of the world, it is my desire to be as completely transparent with you as I can be. I understand that throughout the course of our lives, we will all face the same challenges and anxieties. I want you to know that, no matter where you are, God can reach you and comfort you at any point.

I will use my personal journey and struggles as an example of how powerful and good our God is. I want you to walk resolutely with me as we start the process of allowing God's healing through studying His word and meditating on His divine intervention to transform us spiritually, physically, mentally, and emotionally.

Be encouraged. Dream big. Work hard. Never stop hoping for the best. Keep positive thoughts and believe that we serve an omnipotent God. I dare you to believe the impossible as we journey through this Forty-Day Daily Devotional.

DISCLAIMER

The author does not directly or indirectly dispense medical advice. Nutritionists and others in the field of health hold widely varying views. It is not the intent of this book to diagnose or prescribe. The health tips are a collection of various sources which I have tried and which have worked for me. Only the most common or most widely accepted uses are mentioned. If you decide to diagnose for yourself and use the information without your doctor's approval, you will be prescribing for yourself, but the author assumes no responsibility. The author disclaims liability if the reader uses or prescribes any remedies, natural or otherwise for himself or herself or for another.

Do not be overly encouraged by what may work for others, for it may not work for you as well.

Dr. Author bears no liability if the reader uses or prescribes the remedies in this book, for him/herself or for another.

FOREWORD

Dr. Author has masterfully segued from her first work, *Silent Cry Loud Echo: God Heard Me*, into an epistle that will serve all who have the pleasure of reading it. Regardless of your situation, you will find inspiration, emotional peace, and physical healing in her combination of personal trials and tribulations, biblical wisdom, and natural healing remedies.

In spite of the personal buffeting you might be experiencing from the world, she has crafted forty vignettes and accompanying health strategies to reorient you toward healing (both spiritually and physically) and set you on the path to realizing your true spirit and potential.

I urge you to employ all aspects of her insight, experience, and emotional outpouring. Something within her writings will resonate with you, and you will be so much the better for identifying with her feelings and applying the Scriptural references and healing strategies to your situation.

Enjoy the journey with her. You may be mightily pained by her words, but you will also be uplifted by her inspiration.

JO, 2017

FOREWORD

I have had the extreme pleasure of knowing and working with Dr. Selene Maya Author for over three years. During this time I have witnessed her walk with God and the strength and power of her prayers. Despite the challenges she has had to face and the ups and downs of life, she has remained in love with God and on fire for His kingdom. She is a warm and witty woman who desires nothing more than to help guide people to Christ.

Her first book, *Silent Cry Loud Echo: God Heard Me*, was transformational for all who read it. Her second book, *I Placed My Hands In His: Forty-Day Daily Devotional*, is even more powerful as she gives a word from God and scripture to help the reader grow in his or her walk. Whether you are a babe in Christ or a strong soldier in God's Army this book will renew your faith and strengthen you to continue with God. Rest assured this book will change your life.

—Tonia and Kyra Williams

Be blessed! See you on the other side of the Forty days.

DAY 1

LORD, PUT ME ON YOUR PATH

Sometimes our lives can feel disoriented, the plans we've made have shifted, and suddenly we find ourselves stuck in a place that is dark—a place where we don't want to be. Perhaps you are facing life in prison or caught in financial bankruptcy. Whatever the case is, God will set you free mentally and guide you along your path. Psalm 25:4–5 (NIV) says,

> Show me Your ways, Lord, teach me Your paths.
> Guide me in Your truth and teach me, for You are
> God my Savior, and my hope is in You all day long.

So you may ask, "How do I determine this path and allow Him to guide me on it?" You start by surrendering every area of your life completely to Him, followed by granting Him absolute access to your heart and spirit. The Lord promised that He will show each of us the way of a fulfilled life and allow us to experience the joy of His presence and the pleasures of living with Him forever.

And whatever path we have chosen, we will ultimately end up in the same destination one day if we put God at the forefront. I think the following quote sums it up for us:

> I have not always chosen the safest path. I've made
> my mistakes; plenty of them. I sometimes jump
> too soon and fail to appreciate the consequences.
> But I've learned something important along the
> way: I've learned to heed the call of my heart.
> I've learned that the safest path is not always the
> best path and I've learned that the voice of fear is
> not always to be trusted. (Life Support System.
> Steve Goodier - http://stevegoodier.blogspot.
> com/2013/09/)

One way of hearing from God is by fasting and praying. Usually when fasting, people choose to abstain from food, television, or anything that is sacrilegious or seems to take the place of God in their lives.

The Lord is calling us to make a bold stand and to sacrifice our fleshly desires for a spiritual breakthrough. He said in His word,

> When you fast, do not look somber as the hypocrites
> do, for they disfigure their faces to show others they
> are fasting. Truly I tell you, they have received their
> reward in full. But when you fast, put oil on your
> head and wash your face, so that it will not be ob-
> vious to others that you are fasting, but only to your
> Father, who is unseen; and your Father, who sees
> what is done in secret, will reward you. (Matthew
> 6:16–18 (NIV)

Although fasting is one aspect, please remember that prayer and meditation are equally as important, if not more. Prayer is the conversation you have with God, and meditation is the quiet and the stillness needed to hear God's response. I have learned these three practices—fasting, praying, and meditation—are synonymous with hearing from God.

> Moses was there with the Lord forty days and forty
> nights without eating bread or drinking water. And
> he wrote on the tablets the words of the covenant—
> the Ten Commandments. (Exodus 34:28 NIV)

Over the years, many great men and women of God have testified to the need of including prayer with fasting. John Wesley, a renowned evangelist of the eighteenth century who founded Methodism, placed great emphasis on the practice of fasting and urged other Methodists to follow his lead by fasting every Wednesday and Friday. Though not always easy, fasting is seen as a way to humble ourselves before God.

There will always be mental, physical, and emotional battles to face in this life, but the outcome sought is a need to be filled and an urge to draw closer to Christ the King. And isn't it comforting to know when you fast and pray that you should expect God to move right along with you? If you believe that He can do the impossible, He will.

Before I could embark upon this forty-day journey, I fasted and prayed for confirmation and clarification that writing this book was His will. I would like to share with you my conversation with God.

> Dear Jesus, as I begin this journey, I need to hear
> Your voice as I seek Your face. Let every word that
> I hear from You be expressed on these pages as a
> message of hope and transformation and, most of
> all, a word from You for guidance. Lord, we are all

lost souls without You, and we need You desperately. Times are difficult. And as Your children, we are all encountering differing trials and hardships, at different times and places. We need Your protective arms wrapped around us, protecting us from our travails, hardships, and turmoil. There are those of us who confront the constant temptations of this world, causing us to be pulled in a million directions. Sometimes life gets to be too burdensome. Teach us Your way, Lord, and put us on Your path. Lead us into the destiny You have preordained for us. I trust You, God, that together we will reap the full benefit of this experience, and we will feel Your presence working for our good and for the good of Your kingdom.

In Jesus's holy name. Amen!

Let us be determined to follow His path. Isaiah 58:9 (NIV) says,

Then you will call, and the Lord will answer; you will cry for help, and He will say, "Here am I. If you do away with the yoke of oppression, with the pointing finger, and malicious talk."

People, this walk with God is not an easy life, but it is a rewarding one.

The Lord had said to Abram, "Go from your country, your people, and your father's household to the land I will show you. I will make you into a great nation, and I will bless you; I will make your name great, and you will be a blessing."

Are we willing to follow His directions in order to reap the reward of our obedience?

God always honors His promises. He made what seemed to be impossible possible. No matter how old you might be, God can still use you and perform miracles in your life. Our Father loves us, and even when we might fall to the temptations of the world and make less than godly choices, He is still waiting with open arms ready to receive us, no condemnation whatsoever.

I recall in Exodus that an entire nation of people walked across the floor of the sea, with the raging waters on both sides parted by the power of God. How incredible! God will stop at nothing to save us.

I understand that even in the best of circumstances, life by itself is exceptionally hard to navigate, particularly when one has family responsibilities. Consider the burden laid on Moses's shoulders to lead the Israelites to the Promised Land. When the tribes of Israel were closely pursued at the rear by the Pharaoh's army and at the front by a daunting sea, the fear of failure must have been palpable and the achievement of God's will insurmountable. But steadfastly Moses maintained his faith in God, and He came through for the nation; they made it safely across and their pursuers were swallowed up by the sea. Our Lord can handle what seems to be the impossible and turn it into the possible; we must trust in Him when it seems there is no way.

Margaret D. Nadauld said,

> Your heavenly Father will help you find the right path as you seek His guidance. Remember though, after you pray, you must get off your knees and start

doing something positive; head in the right direction! He will send people along the way who will assist you, but you must be doing your part as well.

Pray this prayer:

My beloved Father, I am in need of Your direction in my life today. Direct my steps so that I may not dash my foot against a stone. You promised to never leave me, and I believe You. I thank You, for as I trust in You completely. You will lead me down Your paths.

In Jesus's name. Amen.

Do You Believe that Your Life Is Lined Up with
the Will of God Our Father? How Can You Make
Changes to Become a Better Version of You?

_____

_____

_____

_____

_____

_____

_____

_____

_____

_____

_____

_____

HEALTH TIP #1: **Drink Your Water Daily!**

In the book *Your Body's Many Cries for Water,* Dr. F. Batmanghelidj said,

> You're not sick; you're thirsty, don't treat thirst with medication. Water has two classic roles in all living matter: Life giving properties, life-sustaining properties.

According to Dr. Batmanghelidj, chronic and persistently increasing dehydration is the root cause of almost all currently encountered major diseases of the human body. He mentioned colitis pain, false appendicitis pain, hiatal hernia, rheumatoid arthritis, low back pain, headaches, stress and depression, and brain function, just to name a few. Drinking water calms nerves, satisfies hunger, cleanses the body, and helps balance pH. In my private practice, usually I too find that people with major health issues do not drink much water.

How much water should one drink daily? According to the Mayo Clinic, no single formula fits everyone. Knowing more about your body's need for fluids will help you estimate how much water to drink each day.

The best type to drink is naturally filtered, mineral-rich water from wells, natural springs, and underground mineral-water reservoirs. These types of water contain minerals, such as potassium, sodium, and magnesium, which are vital for helping your body perform optimally.

Adding liquid chlorophyll to your water adds to its healing properties, as it has the ability to bind and remove toxic heavy metals like mercury from your body. It also helps bad breath and digestive issues. Liquid chlorophyll is one of my personal favorites. I hope you enjoy.

DAY 2

LORD, IT'S YOUR CHILD ONCE AGAIN

I come to You, my beloved Father, desperately seeking Your face for guidance and answers. You alone can heal me and love me like no one else can. Show me where to walk so that my feet may not stumble. Lord pour out your blessing so that I am planted on firm grounds. Help me in times of despair—replace heartaches with hope. Allow me to feel your presence in times of loneliness and do not allow the trials of life to prevail against me. For you are all powerful, my beginning and my end is in Your hands. I am on bended knees, Lord. Pour out Your blessings upon me, my children and my family.

I have been waking up daily to do my morning prayers at 3:00 a.m. for many years now. And although it's an early hour, I normally feel the spirit of joy because the presence of God is evident from the peace and tranquility that is in the atmosphere. This gives me a relief from the cares of this world. Many times I find myself in the presence of God for hours. It's my safe place.

I remember that during the storms of my life, God comforted me. He showed me repeatedly that He is an ever present help in times of need.

I take comfort in Psalm 46:1–2 (NIV): "God is our refuge and strength, an ever-present help in trouble. Therefore, we will not fear, though the earth give way and the mountains fall into the heart of the sea." This is so profound. It seems as if there is always flooding or a natural disaster going on. Yet He comforts us giving us hope that He is indeed our ever present help in times of trouble.

We clearly see that, whatever situations we have endured or will encounter presently or in the future, God is with us. At one particular point in my life, I had a very difficult time sleeping. I tossed and turned, but the minute I began to pray, I could feel God's presence, and there came over me a peace and comfort that I couldn't explain. Sleep would then come to me, and I would rest peacefully until daybreak.

Whatever our circumstances might be, we can always find strength in the word of God. Those who listen to the word find something stronger than themselves to lean on and can draw their strength from that. You are indeed the apple of God's eye, and whatever might concern you also concerns Him. If you are one who has grown up in a negative environment and were told repeatedly that you will never be anything, I sympathize; nevertheless, it's time to come out of that defeatist mentality.

In Hebrews 4:15 (NIV), Jesus said, "For we do not have a high priest who is unable to empathize with our weakness, but we have one who has been tempted in every way, just as we are, yet He did not sin."

Imagine that: how much your Father loves and cares for you that He not only gave His life so that we could live, but also that He understands our very groans that are too deep for words! There's nothing greater than the love that the Father has for us, so therefore I encourage you to be not faint of heart in seeking His intercession.

In Matthew 7:7–11 (NIV), the Bible says, "Ask and it will be given to you; seek and you will find; knock and the door will be opened to you. For everyone who asks receives; the one who seeks finds; and to the one who knocks, the door will be opened. Which of you, if your son asks for bread, will give him a stone? Or if he asks for a fish, will give him a snake? If you, then, though you are evil, know how to give good gifts to your children, how much more will your Father in heaven give good gifts to those who ask him!"

Dear friends, as we embark upon this forty-day walk with God, I pray that He will speak to us and teach us who He is in a real and personal way. I also write this in the hope that you will challenge yourselves in the areas that I spoke about to provoke growth in order to see yourself as God sees you and to reassure yourselves that all things are possible through Christ who strengthens us.

God is able to change your course because He is the author and finisher of your life story. Do not remain in doom and gloom. God is always at hand—all you have to do is call upon Him. It is my hope that you will learn to trust Him. Trust Him with your whole heart, you will never go wrong!

What Are You Asking God for? You Must Be Clear.

_____

_____

_____

_____

_____

_____

_____

_____

_____

_____

_____

_____

HEALTH TIP # 2: **Get Eight to Ten Hours of Sleep**

Sleep deprivation can lead to insomnia, a restlessness or an inability to fall or stay asleep, which can lead to dysfunction in everyday life.

Some of the main causes of insomnia are irregular work hours, stress, loss of a job or loved ones, and eating the evening meal too close to bedtime. There are also several medical conditions that contribute to the development of insomnia: asthma, hypothyroidism, fibromyalgia, and mood disorders.

Though insomnia is very common, affecting more than one-third of the population at least once, it is found more often in adult women than in any other group. Additionally, it is estimated that at least 10 percent of the population suffers from chronic or repeated insomnia.

A lack of sleep can weaken the immune system, disrupt brain function, and can impair cognitive abilities, which in turn can cause a higher risk of accidents. This can lead to not only physical but also mental and emotional health setbacks.

Mixing lavender and chamomile essential oil and rubbing it under the feet can enhance relaxation before sleep, leading to a better night's rest.

DAY 3

WORSHIP YOUR WAY TO VICTORY

In years past, I was never ashamed to run up to the altar, drop to my knees, and worship God. I knew in my heart that He is all I have, and I needed Him to help me make my way through the trials of life, so I worshiped Him publicly. I was never too embarrassed to confess Jesus as my savior.

I recall an earlier time when I was abandoned and alone with young children. I had never before worked outside the home and had exhausted all my funds on attorney fees. This was done in hopes that I would receive some kind of support for us.

At the time, I found myself penniless and with no food in my house. So naturally I was in a crisis mode, and a severe panic attack began to overwhelm me. I literally felt like I could not breathe; I remember falling to the kitchen floor, panting for breath. Lying on the floor, I cried out to God. "God, please do not allow me to die this way. Save me by your power."

I began to pray, and I heard the Lord say to me, "Don't you trust me?"

I immediately answered, "Yes, Lord!" My brothers and sisters, I felt a warm embrace and the panic attack instantly left.

I gathered my Bible and went into my closet (my war room), and I began to pray and worship the Lord. I cried out and He heard me! By the end of that day, a mother from the church I attended had come by with her arms full of bags of food! She said, "Baby girl, God told me to bring you groceries!"

Not only did she bring me groceries, but my best friend also brought me groceries too! By the end of the day, I had so many groceries that I couldn't close my refrigerator, and I had things lined up all across my countertop. In Psalm 34:17 (NIV), the Bible says, "The righteous cry out, and the Lord hears them; He delivers them from all their troubles." The key word here in this scripture is *all*. The Lord said that He will deliver us out of all of our troubles, not some. Trust Him!

On another occasion, I was faced with the daunting task of having to mow fifteen acres of grass. I had no idea how on earth I would do this, but God sent me help and I learned to do it myself. When I started working full time, I could not be home to cut all that grass, nor could I afford to hire someone to cut it for me. It would have cost a lot of money, but God sent me someone who volunteered to cut my grass for free. This blessing stayed in my life for three and a half years. When that blessed man could no longer help, God sent me someone else. He initially wanted to be paid but later told me that God told him not to charge me.

Only God knows your inner cries. Trust me: He cares!

It's amazing that there is something most special about the name Jesus. All you have to do is call upon Him, and His grace and healing will occur. God wants us to show the breadth of our faithfulness and trust in Him, even in the midst of turmoil and hardships. He wants us to trust Him completely no matter what the situation.

Hallelujah! Glory to His name! The power of your praise

will determine the magnitude of your breakthrough. Praise him today!

However, in spite of His goodness, God will often test your faith. Paul and Silas didn't wait until they'd received a breakthrough or miracle for them to praise and show their thankfulness to God. In the midst of their trials, they praised God, and He gave them the breakthrough they so desired.

Acts 16:25–26 (NIV) states, "About midnight, Paul and Silas were praying and singing hymns to God, and the other prisoners were listening to them. Suddenly there was such a violent earthquake that the foundations of the prison were shaken. At once all the prison doors flew open, and everyone's chains came loose."

Even through pain and suffering, Paul and Silas praised God. Despite the hardships they faced, they continued with their praise, and as a result, God came through for them in a miraculous way.

We were created to worship and praise God, and the closer you grow to Him, the more natural it should be for you to express your love for Him.

WORSHIP THE LORD YOUR GOD WITH ALL YOUR SOUL AND ALL YOUR MIGHT

"Rejoice in the Lord always. I will say it again: Rejoice! Let your gentleness be evident to all. The Lord is near. Do not be anxious about anything, but in everything, by prayer and petition, with thanksgiving, present your requests to God. And the peace of God, which transcends all understanding, will guard your hearts and your minds in Christ Jesus" (Philippians 4:4 NIV).

In Colossians 3:14–17 (NIV), Paul said, "And above all these put on love, which binds everything together in perfect harmony. And let the peace of Christ rule in your hearts, to which indeed you were called in one body. And be thankful. Let the word of Christ dwell in you richly, teaching and admonishing one another in all wisdom, singing psalms and hymns and spiritual songs, with thankfulness in your hearts to God. And whatever you do, in word or deed, do everything in the name of the Lord Jesus, giving thanks to God the Father through Him."

Throughout my life I have journeyed through valleys and encountered abysses and ravines. I have endured throughout, and although I have had to come face-to-face with the worst, I also have had the pleasure to experience many great things. My life has been a great panorama of experiences, but through it all, I always knew I was never alone. I believe God and His word.

Our beloved Father's comforting words to us, "So do not worry, saying, 'What shall we eat?' or 'What shall we drink?' or 'What shall we wear?' For the pagans run after all these things, and your heavenly Father knows that you need them. But seek first His kingdom and His righteousness, and all these things will be given to you as well. Therefore do not worry about tomorrow, for tomorrow will worry about itself. Each day has enough trouble of its own" (Matthew 6:31–34 NIV). What a great revelation! He understands our troubles, so He comforts us by reassuring us that He acknowledges that "each day has enough trouble of its own"

I often picture this scene: Jesus talking to his disciples and telling them to quit their jobs, leave their homes, and follow him—to not be afraid. He told them, "Do not worry about your life, what you will eat; or about your body, what you will wear. For life is more than food, and the body more than clothes." Can you see yourself here with Jesus?

In John 14:27 (NIV), the Bible says, "Peace I leave with you; My peace I give you. I do not give to you as the world gives. Do not let your hearts be troubled and do not be afraid." Oh how I love the word of the Lord! Trust and believe, my beloved!

Do You Need God to Make a Way Out of No Way?

What are the things you will lay at His feet?

_____

_____

_____

_____

_____

_____

_____

_____

_____

_____

_____

_____

HEALTH TIP #3: **Cooking for Health**

Proper combination of ingredients can enhance the assimilation of vital nutrients and help avoid digestion difficulties. However, discovering the proper combinations can be a complicated process.

There are a few basic guidelines that will help you in your quest:

1. Do not combine protein with starches.
2. Do not combine fruits and vegetables at the same time.
3. It is beneficial to eat fruits on an empty stomach and not concurrently with other foods.
4. Do not consume multiple proteins within the same meal. An example would be having hamburger and chicken in one meal—switch one of the meats out for a beneficial vegetable, like onions or spinach.
5. Do not drink liquids with meals. Wait for at least thirty minutes before and after each meal.

DAY 4

FAITH AS A MUSTARD SEED

At one point in my life, I must admit, I allowed fear to engulf my mind. I was in the midst of a terrible situation. I was told that we had to move out of our home. We had been in the house for many years by this time, and my children had become accustomed to the neighborhood, the school, and their friends. We were also left without any reliable form of transportation. Difficult times were surely staring me in the face.

I didn't even know how I would get my kids back and forth to school, as we lived in a rural area with long country roads, and it was quite a drive to the bus stop. The ensuing turmoil, fear, and dread seemed almost too much for me to bear. Mentally, I was exhausted, but I knew that God had come through for me in the past and He would not leave or forsake me now. Miraculous to say, one of my friends came through and took my children to school until I got proper transportation. My faith kept me in perfect sanity. God is on time!

What my beloved friend did was simply divine. God used her to bless me and my children. What a kind gesture that was. It was exactly what was needed and had arrived at the perfect time. My God is an on-time God. Sometimes in life, your immediate family won't extend a helping hand, but a kind friend or stranger will.

I asked God to shield and protect me and my children from harm and to allow us to keep our home. He did just that, allowing us to stay there until they finished high school and beyond. I promise you that if you exercise your faith in Jesus, His power and glory will blow your mind. The Bible says that when the enemy comes in like a flood, God will raise up a standard for you.

What I'm saying is that sometimes we go into panic mode for no justifiable reason. We obsess on our current situation, allowing it to consume our bodies and spirits and bombard us, causing major health issues.

We are called to trust in God and not doubt Him. I know now that it may be difficult sometimes to put your faith in God and trust Him to work out the situation when the world around you is collapsing. But believe me; I am living proof of the power of God. I am proof that no pit is so deep that Jesus can't reach in and pull you out. Ask yourself, ***Can my faith sustain me to victory?***

I pray that out of His glorious riches He may strengthen you with power through His Spirit so that Christ may dwell in your hearts through faith. And I pray that you remain rooted and established in His love, that you have the courage to stand firm and trust Him for yourself.

Ephesians 3:16–17 (NIV) states, "May the God of hope fill you with all joy and peace as you trust in Him, so that you may overflow with hope by the power of the Holy Spirit."

In Romans 15:13 (NIV), Paul said, "Though you have not seen Him, you love Him; and even though you do not see Him now, you believe in Him and are filled with an inexpressible and glorious joy, for you are receiving the end result of your faith, the salvation of your souls."

In 1 Peter 1:8–9 (NIV), the Bible says, "Jesus said to her, 'I am the resurrection and the life. The one who believes in me will live, even though they die; and whoever lives by believing in me will never die.'"

We must fight the good fight and remain strong by holding onto our faith in Jesus. Choose to stand strong in faith even when you see no end in sight to your situation. Press forward through the hardships and discomfort that comes with believing in what your eyes can't see. Despite what others may say, do not allow fear to overtake you. Allow your Father to embrace you and in return He will build and strengthen your faith in Him.

Revelation 14:12 (NIV) says, "This calls for patient endurance on the part of the saints who obey God's commandments and remain faithful to Jesus."

Never stop praying for strength and guidance. He hears our prayers and knows our every need. As I said earlier, pray and worship God through the hardships, and He will guide your footsteps. He will renew your strength. Pray through the temptation to stray. "Watch and pray, so that you will not fall into temptation. The spirit is willing, but the body is weak" (Matthew 26:41 NIV).

Even if you do fall to temptation, start again. God is always there for you, even when you fall.

In order to empower yourself, you must become familiar with the scripture and the word of God. It is food for our souls. It will give you wisdom, knowledge, and understanding and will establish boldness in your soul. When the weight of the world becomes too much, bury yourself in His word. Stay among people who can help you up through the tough times. Open your Bible, visit a church, or call up a friend to pray for you—anything that will help you keep yourself on track.

Is Your Lack of Faith Setting You on a Path to Defeat?

HEALTH TIP #4: **Purchase Organic Foods**

- Organically grown vegetables are more beneficial in that they lack chemicals that, over time, may harm you.
- All types of root vegetables, like carrots, celery, and turnips, absorb more toxins from the soil than vegetables grown above ground.
- Peel all fruits and vegetables that are not organically grown.
- Replace sugar with xylitol, a natural sweetener, in your cooking and baking. It has no clear signs of effect on blood sugar or insulin levels and also has less calories than regular sugar. You can get xylitol at most health food stores.

DAY 5

THE POWER OF PRAYER

There was a time when I needed the intervention of God to heal a family member. At the time, he was just about eight months old, and I feared for his life because of the condition he was struggling with. The doctors could do nothing about it. One Sunday, in desperation, I literally placed him on the altar, got on my knees in front of him, and pleaded with God to heal him. I wasn't sure if God could have healed him instantly; nevertheless, I believed that God would do it for us. He was helpless as he was only eight months old.

Surely enough, God did what I had beseeched Him to do! He healed this precious child. Our God is powerful and He answers prayers!

The power of prayer should not be underestimated. In James 5:16 (NIV), the Bible says, "The prayer of a righteous man is powerful and effective."

In 1 John 5:14–15 (NIV), the Bible also says, "This is the confidence we have approaching God: that if we ask anything according to His will, He hears us. And if we know that He heard us—whatever we ask—we know that we have what we asked of Him."

God knows our hearts, and it does not matter who is praying—He takes us all seriously! He answers all prayers that are in agreement with His will. Although His answers may not always be yes, believe in your heart that He knows all our needs and wants, and He will give to us according to His desires.

Please understand that when we pray earnestly, sincerely, and purposefully, according to His will, God hears our cries and will respond powerfully.

PRAY WITHOUT CEASING. PRAY NIGHT AND DAY. GOD IS LISTENING!

Matthew 7:7–8 (NIV) says, "Ask and it will be given to you; seek and you will find; knock and the door will be opened to you. For everyone who asks receives; he who seeks finds; and to him who knocks, the door will be opened. Thus saith our God!"

It is said so passionately in Isaiah 30:19 (NIV): "O people of Zion, who live in Jerusalem, you will weep no more. How gracious He will be when you cry for help! As soon as He hears, He will answer you." To God be the glory!

My beloved friends, it doesn't get better than this: we have a God who is mighty in strength and loves us unconditionally in spite of our sins and shortcomings. Wow!

In the book of Jeremiah 29:12 (NIV), the Lord God Almighty said, "Then you will call upon me and come and pray to me, and I will listen to you."

In John 16:23–24 (NIV), the Bible states, "In that day you will no longer ask Me anything. I tell you the truth, my Father will give you whatever you ask in My name. Until now, you have not asked for anything in My name. Ask and you will receive, and your joy will be complete."

It fascinates me what God is saying to us in so many words and in so many scriptures: Just ask, and it will be done for you! Knock and the door will open.

One of my favorite verses in the Bible, Psalm 50:15 (NIV), says, "And call upon Me in the day of trouble; I will deliver you, and you will honor Me."

The Lord speaks with authority and confidence, and He wants us to do the same; He does not want us to be a weak people and nation. He gives us clear instructions and a guide to follow in any circumstances we encounter.

Psalm 145:18–19 (NIV) proclaims, "The Lord is near to all who call on Him, to all who call on Him in truth. He fulfills the desires of those who fear Him; He hears their cry and saves them."

People of God, stand still and firm in your faith. God is with you. If God is for you, then who can be against you?

In Zechariah 13:9 (NIV) Jesus reassures us that even in the fire He will set a watch over us: "This third will I bring into the fire; I will refine them like silver and test them like gold. They will call on My name and I will answer them; I will say 'They are my people," and they will say, 'The Lord is our God.'" And in Jeremiah 33:3 (NIV), He continues, "Call to me and I will answer you and tell you great and unsearchable things you do not know."

This is my prayer for you.

God will enlarge your territory and bless you with increase in all aspects of your life. He will bestow divine favor on you in Jesus's name.

What is Your Deepest Desire? Tell God! Pour Out Your Heart to Him!

_____

_____

_____

_____

_____

_____

_____

_____

_____

_____

_____

_____

HEALTH TIP # 5: **Read Labels and Shop Smart**

- Read the labels on the foods you buy carefully. Stay away from foods that have a long list of nonfood ingredients, like chemicals, artificial colorings, additives, and so on. The first ingredient on the label lists the one in the largest/primary amount. Note carefully the amount of salt and sugar present.

- Do most of your shopping on the perimeter of the grocery store. The perimeter is where fruits, vegetables, dairy, and fresh fish and meat are sold. These are the foods that are the most beneficial for you. The center aisles of the store normally contain the processed and junk food that should be avoided.

- Never use white distilled vinegar during cooking or on salads. Use only apple cider vinegar. This is good for calming heartburn and enhancing healthy cholesterol, and can aid in weight loss and more. Start with a small amount and gradually work your way to taking, at most, two tablespoons per day.

DAY 6

FORGIVE AND FREE YOURSELF

I truly became free on the day I realized that God's forgiveness was for the betterment of me, and not to those who hurt me. Through my experiences, I discovered that long-held unforgiveness, bitterness, and pain kept me captive and contributed to my sorrow.

I was searching for answers to the hurt I felt inside. I didn't understand how someone who claimed to love me, swore to honor and protect me, could be the very person that tore my heart apart. I will never forget the day that I attended a conference on forgiveness and the speaker began to tell his story. I was amazed because his story resonated with mine. That day, he said something that changed my habit of harboring bitterness and unforgiveness.

What he said was so simple yet so very profound. He said that God died for that person who had hurt me and that He loved them too. I am not sure why those few words had such a great impact on my life, but I do believe that if Jesus can forgive his accusers, who am I not to?

Every one of us has experienced some kind of pain and hurt in the form of bodily injury, sexual abuse, or mental or psychological mistreatment. Whatever form it might be, you can either hold onto the anger, resentment, and vengeful thoughts or you can embrace forgiveness and move forward with your life.

My friends, even though the act of forgiveness may be difficult, I urge you to make that decision to let go of resentment and hatred. I understand that perhaps what happened to you may always remain a part of your life, but forgiveness can lessen its grip on you. For me, I wasn't able to forgive until I released the anger I felt within.

I recall that, on the day I chose to forgive, I developed empathy and compassion for those who had hurt me.

Don't get me wrong; forgiveness doesn't mean that you deny the other person's responsibility for hurting you, and it doesn't minimize or justify the wrongdoing. It is unfortunate that this happened, but look to Jesus for your strength. He extends a loving invitation for forgiveness of sins which is only possible through His shed blood; He gave His life so that we may live. We are forgiven because He was forsaken. His amazing love for us is like no other. Choose to forgive and allow your heavenly Father's love to cover you!

Isaiah 55:6–7 (NIV) says, "Seek the Lord while He may be found; call upon Him while He is near. Let the wicked forsake His way and the evil man His thoughts. Let him return to the Lord, and He will have mercy on him, and to our God, for He will freely pardon."

In Matthew 11:28–30 (NIV), Jesus said, "Come to me, all who are weary and burdened, and I will give you rest. Take My yoke upon you and learn from Me, for I am gentle and humble in heart, and you will find rest for your souls. For My yoke is easy and My burden is light."

In 2 Corinthians 2:5–8 (NIV), the Bible states, "If anyone has caused grief, he has not so much grieved Me as he has grieved all of you, to some extent - not to put it too severely. The punishment inflicted on him by the majority is sufficient for him. Now instead, you ought to forgive and comfort him, so that he will not be overwhelmed by excessive sorrow. I urge you, therefore, to reaffirm your love for him."

So remember: to forgive someone is one of the highest, most admirable forms of God's love within you. Imagine forgiving the person that wounded you and letting them know you've forgiven them. To withhold forgiveness means you continue to remain the victim of the hurt.

As a doctor of natural medicine, I've seen a spirit of unforgiveness manifest itself in major health issues such as weakened immune systems, chemical imbalances, depression, and increased stress. Some of the physical consequences are a weakened immune system, chemical and hormone balance, and lack of sleep. It causes depression, adds stress, and creates bitterness and resentment inside the body. Not only that but also it can cause a strain on your relationship with God and hinder spiritual development.

Choose to Free Yourself!

Who Do You Need to Forgive?

_____

_____

_____

_____

_____

_____

_____

_____

_____

_____

_____

_____

HEALTH TIP #6: **Put Yourself on a Path to Wellness**

- Cleanse and detoxify your body on a regular basis. A good way to start is by drinking water daily and being conscious of the foods you put in your body. This enhances overall health and wellness.
- Select and take the appropriate nutritional supplements such as a whole food vitamin and mineral, essential fatty acids, and food enzymes.
- Liquid multivitamins are highly recommended because your digestive systems absorbs the plant-derived liquid nutrients faster than tablets.

DAY 7

HIS GRACE IS SUFFICIENT

There have been times in my life where I felt as though I had reached rock bottom. Everything around me seemed to be coming apart, and I felt that there was nothing I could do about it. In spite of my seasons of despair, my faith in God continued to remain strong for I knew deep inside that my Lord would never leave nor forsake me as long as I could hang on to the hem of His garment. I pleaded with God to deliver me and give me a second wind.

Then He reminded me of the story of Job, and He said in a soft, sweet whisper, "My grace is sufficient for you." Oh how I love this! To me these words are like a love song in my ear.

Job was a believer who loved God, and yet God allowed Satan to torment Job to such a degree that he started to despair in his own life and rue the day he was born. He had lost everything - everyone had left him, his friends had turned against him. His wife even told him to curse God and die. Still, Job continued to serve God. When you believe that you have reached your end, think about Job: he lost his children, his wealth, his health, his crops, and his livestock. This was everything he had! The people believed his suffering was caused by his sins. Job even felt as if God had turned his back on him. Oh, how he must have suffered!

In Job 23:2–4 (NIV), the scripture says, "Even today, my complaint is bitter; His hand is heavy in spite of my groaning. If only I knew where to find Him; if only I could go to His dwelling! I would state my case before Him and fill my mouth with arguments."

At so many times in my life, I've felt like Job. If I could have seen Jesus in front of me, I probably would also cry out to Him and beg to plead my case. The good news, my friends, is we can cry out to Him and do just that. It's natural to question God just like Job did, but like Job, we must not allow our desolate situation to consume us. This is not an easy life but your Father knows all.

Job repented and was humbled before God. Our God is truly amazing; He restored Job and He will do the same for us.

Job 42:10 (NIV) says, "After Job had prayed for his friends, the Lord restored his fortunes and gave him twice as much as he had before."

In Psalm 142:1–2 (NIV), the Bible states, "I cry aloud to the Lord; I lift up my voice to the Lord for mercy. I pour out before Him my complaint; before Him I tell my trouble." Here we find that God wants us to forgive and go to Him with our cares.

We will always have struggle as long as there is breath in our bodies, but our struggles are not all the same. But despite all, I am here to tell you that there is no faith worth having that has not been tested by fire. Allow your struggles to strengthen your walk with Jesus. Pray without ceasing, and God will give you the grace to endure. Accept His grace—it's free!

You may ask, "What is grace?" It is God showing His love to us even though we certainly don't deserve it. We cannot earn

His grace. God shows His grace by giving us the strength to overcome. He loves us unconditionally, and His greatest act of grace is the gift of salvation that is available for all of us through faith.

Ephesians 2:8–9 (NIV) says, "For it is by grace you have been saved, through faith—and this is not from yourselves, it is the gift of God - not by works, so that no one can boast." This great gift is eternal life, a promise of a home one day in heaven with God.

Esther 2:16–17 (NIV) says, "She was taken to King Xerxes in the royal residence in the tenth month, the month of Tebeth, in the seventh year of his reign. Now the king was attracted to Esther more than to any of the other women, and she won his favor and approval more than any of the other virgins. So he set a royal crown on her head and made her queen instead of Vashti." God's favour over our lives can make a great difference.

In Jeremiah 31:2–3 (NIV), the Bible states, "This is what the Lord says: 'The people who survive the sword will find favor in the wilderness; I will come to give rest to Israel.'" The Lord appeared to us in the past, saying: "I have loved you with an everlasting love; I have drawn you with unfailing kindness."

In 2 Corinthians 12:8–9 (NIV), the Bible says, "Three times I pleaded with the Lord to take it away from me. But He said to me, "My grace is sufficient for you, for My power is made perfect in weakness. Therefore I will boast all the more gladly about my weaknesses, so that Christ's power may rest on me." Rest in Jesus—He knows what you are going through.

Hebrews 4:6 (NIV) states, "Let us then with confidence

draw near to the throne of Grace, that we may receive mercy and find grace to help in time of need."

Oh, God, grant me your grace. You alone know my weaknesses and failures, and without your help, I cannot accomplish anything. Lord, give me the strength to face and overcome what is ahead of me. Teach me to bear patiently all the trials of suffering or failure that may come for me today. Amen.

Think of a Time when God Extended His Grace to You and Give Thanks.

_____

_____

_____

_____

_____

_____

_____

_____

_____

_____

_____

_____

HEALTH TIP #7: **Dizziness**

Feelings of dizziness can be caused by high or low blood pressure, anemia, ear problems, and poor cerebral circulation.

The use of the following herbs will help relieve the impact of dizziness:

- Licorice root balances blood sugar levels. It comes in both liquid and capsule form, though I personally recommend liquid form.
- Ginger, which is a digestive aid, can be made into tea from both the powdered and raw forms. I personally prefer fresh ginger.
- Ginkgo/gotu kola helps supply oxygen to the brain.
- Butcher's broom or capsicum increases circulation. I keep liquid Capsicum on me at all times. Whenever I feel a chest pain I squeeze several drops in my mouth and for a while I took it for about six months. It helps me!

DAY 8

FIND STRENGTH IN JESUS

We cannot avoid suffering, but I urge you to seek God's word through learning and studying. And as you study, you too will grow in strength and in faith.

Today, as I think on God and I seek His face while studying His word, Joshua 1:9 (NIV) comes to mind. God said, "Have I not commanded you? Be strong and courageous. Do not be afraid; do not be discouraged, for the Lord your God will be with you wherever you go."

This is God talking directly to us. In this scripture, He is encouraging us to be strong and is reminding us that He is with us. In so many ways and in so many scriptures, He encourages us and time and again reassures us that He will be with us through it all.

Many times in my life I was so mentally drained that I literally felt that I could not pray. The only word I could utter was, "Jesus." When you find yourself in that place where you just don't feel that you have the strength to pray, trust me, just say, "Jesus," and it will make a world of difference in your life. There is power and strength when you say that name. I have personally experienced it myself.

I specifically recall the time when I was about seventeen. I was not in a place of balance. I was very confused and with no proper direction. Two years prior to this time, I had been living in Guyana, South America, under the protection of my father. Now I found myself on my own in a very dark place. Dealing with trauma as a result of rape, my current world, as I knew it, was dark. All I wanted to do was to be left alone. I just wanted to check out! To make matters worse, this was my secret. I had no friends and no one to talk to.

I recall on my second job one of my coworkers was a Christian and possessed a joy that just got on my nerves. She always made it a point to tell me about her church and encouraged me to visit. It was a very small Pentecostal church in the neighborhood I lived in, and realizing I had nothing to lose, I decided to attend. I told myself that I was not going to say a word to anyone, and I hoped they would return the favor. I took a seat at the very back of the church and kept to myself; to my surprise this little church was overflowing with people. This did not bother me, as no one knew me and I did not see my annoying coworker that night.

Toward the end of the service, the preacher, a very short, powerful woman, began to call people to the altar. I began to pray and asked the Lord, "If you are real, let her call me out personally." At the very minute I finished my prayer, her words entered my soul.

She shouted, "You in the back!" Afraid that she actually was talking to me, I cowered as low as I could get, and told my seatmate that it was he who the pastor, in fact, was calling. Amazingly, it was as if the pastor heard me!

She then said, "I am calling you since you have asked God to point you out, and He did." She told me to come up to the front because God had a word for me. Nervously, I walked up, and the pastor told me, "God is going to use you for great things." She then began to prophesy over me.

My faith in the Lord was ultimately renewed through this, and I gained strength, knowing that Jesus Christ of Nazareth lives!

People of God, surrender your life today! Tomorrow may very well be too late!

Dear friends, I recommend that you turn your life to Jesus Christ as a start in changing your situation. In your times of weakness call upon Him. He will answer as He did for me.

In Psalm 28:7–8 (NIV), the psalmist said, "The Lord is my strength and my shield; my heart trusts in Him, and He helps me. My heart leaps for joy, and with my song I praise him. The Lord is the strength of his people, a fortress of salvation for his anointed one." Isaiah 40:29–31 (NIV) states, "He gives strength to the weary and increases the power of the weak. Even youths grow tired and weary, and young men stumble and fall; but those who hope in the Lord will renew their strength. They will soar on wings like eagles; they will run and not grow weary, they will walk and not be faint."

In Hebrews 4:12 (NIV), the Bible says, "For the word of God is alive and active. Sharper than any double-edged sword, it penetrates even to dividing soul and spirit, joints and marrow; it judges the thoughts and attitudes of the heart." God wants us to have a pure heat.

What Is the Thorn in Your Flesh that
You Need God's Strength to Deal With?
Make a List and Deal with It.

_____

_____

_____

_____

_____

_____

_____

_____

_____

_____

_____

_____

HEALTH TIP #8: **Fever**

A fever is symptomatic of the body trying to burn excess waste. Fevers can be caused by bronchitis, colds, diabetes, chronic infection, influenza, mononucleosis, or rheumatic disorders.

There are a few herbs that will help to treat/minimize the effects of a fever:

- Feverfew, a medicinal plant, is used to reduce fever and cool the body. This, and other plant supplements, can be taken in either capsule, liquid, or tea forms.
- Lobelia, a plant derivative, can be used both internally and externally to help calm a fever
- Yarrow, another plant-derived herb, is commonly used to induce perspiration and break a fever.
- Drinking larger amounts of fluids also helps to keep the body hydrated as it burns off waste

DAY 9

LEAN ON GOD'S MERCY

As I write this devotional today, I feel as if God is continuing to test me through the topics and insights I've been detailing. So from my heart to yours, I will be as transparent as I possibly can.

On this one particular day, I felt especially burdened with the cares of life. Physically, I just felt exhausted. I found myself wanting to talk to a friend. I dialed a few of my closest friends, but to my disappointment, none of them were available. As I sat in my car and cried, unsure of who to turn to, I suddenly recalled a pastor who had promised to mentor me, one of many who had offered to help in such way. Nevertheless, I choose this one particular one because he seemed kind and understanding. I remembered that he'd prayed a powerful prayer that shook me, and I knew I had to speak with him. I reached out to him, telling him that I needed prayer because everything around me seemed to be falling apart.

I thought I needed a man of God to pray for me in order to witness and inspire change. My brother—we will call him Pastor Gumpfree—listened to me for a short while and then said, "I will need fifteen hundred dollars to help you, because this is a ministry too."

Shocked, I replied to him, "Pastor Gumpfree, I am having financial difficulties too."

He replied, "Okay. I will take one thousand instead. Go and pray tonight and ask God where you can get the money from. Then just let me know when you have it." I was completely taken aback by his response and felt worse than ever when I got off the phone.

My spirit was particularly grieved in this, which made me realize my body and mind were not in agreement. Therefore, I knew in my heart that I was not supposed to oblige.

Thankfully, I know my true identity in Christ. I could not and would not allow his callous and greedy response to completely crush my spirits and spin me off into new cares and despairs.

How many of you can relate to this situation? The feeling that you've been taken advantage of by someone in a position of authority and prestige. I understand giving to the man of God and sewing a seed in his life, but this did not rest well in my spirit.

It was at that moment, I found myself asking, "God, is that decision alright with you?" God then told me that some pastors are not walking by His Spirit and instead are focusing on their fleshly bodies and monetary needs. This causes them to take advantage of His people and their needs, which is a sin. Immediately, I prayed for God's mercy upon the pastor and myself.

In Psalm 51:1 (NIV), David cried out to God, "Have mercy on me, O God, according to your unfailing love; according to your great compassion, blot out my transgressions."

This situation grieved my soul for many days after that, and it continues to upset my spirit to this day. You have no need to pay another person so that you can proceed on a path to God—you can call Him directly through prayer. God will direct you in such decisions.

Thankfully, I had found God for myself, and I know that scripture says, "God is our refuge and strength, an ever-present help in trouble" (Psalm 46:1 NIV).

My brothers and sisters, if a man or woman of the cloth has ever wounded and disappointed you, I challenge you to forgive him or her and allow God to lead you into your God-given destiny. Remember that in your desolate times, God is ever-present. You can call upon Him, and He will be right there for you.

Our God is certainly a God of mercy. When He appeared to Moses in Exodus 34:6 (NIV), He declared His name before Moses in these words: "The Lord, the Lord, the compassion-ate and gracious God, slow to anger, abounding in love and faithfulness."

My beloved God is merciful and filled with compassion. Remember, people of God, that your Father's eyes can see through the whole earth!

God sees and hears your cries. Cry out to Jesus and not to man. Only God can make your situation right and ease your heart's pain. "Blessed are the merciful, for they will be shown mercy" (Matthew 5:7 NIV).

Jude 1:22–23 (NIV) states, "Be merciful to those who doubt; save others by snatching them from the fire; to others show mercy, mixed with fear—hating even the clothing stained by corrupted flesh." And God will let you know in your spirit what is not right. There are many good Preachers that are ready and willing to reach out.

In Luke 10:37 (NIV), the Bible says, "Which of these three do you think was a neighbor to the man who fell into the hands of robbers?" The expert in the law replied, 'The one who had mercy on him.' Jesus told him, 'Go and do likewise.'"

Extending mercy is one of the most powerful ways we demonstrate the character of Christ to each other.

Dear Father, today I need You to extend Your mercy to me in every aspect of my life so that I can be kind and merciful to someone in need. Help me to sense the needs of another and be quick without hesitation to lend a helping hand. May I be like pliable clay in the potter's hand. I permit You, most holy one, to shape me into the person You would have me be. Use me for Your people, in Your way, in Your time, for Your glory. In Jesus's name I pray. Amen.

In What Ways Do You Extend Mercy to Your Brothers and Sisters?

_____

_____

_____

_____

_____

_____

_____

_____

_____

_____

_____

_____

HEALTH TIP #9: **Eat Pomegranate**

Pomegranate is a sweet fruit that is rich in antioxidants, vitamins, minerals, and fibers. Some benefits of pomegranate include the following:

1. It protects your skin by aiding cell regeneration and tissue repair as well as improving circulation, which aids in the healing of wounds
2. It protects your skin from damage caused by prolonged exposure to the sun. It is also known to help fight skin cancer.
3. Pomegranate helps prevent wrinkles, fine lines, age spots, and hyperpigmentation. This fruit should be consumed at least three times weekly along with berries, bananas, pineapple. Get into the habit of eating fruits and vegetables daily. Cut back on meats if possible.

DAY 10

MY PEACE I GIVE UNTO YOU

For many years, I had seen this older gentleman on the streets of the town where I live. This kind old man seemed to be in his eighties, and he had lived on the streets for years. Every now and then, the local churches would give him shelter, but most of the time he lived behind a grocery store in a tent. He always had a smile on his face, and seemed joyful despite his circumstances. One day I decided to stop and talk to him, and before I knew it, we became friends.

One evening my friend walked into my business and said to me, "It's getting ready to storm, and I don't want to be caught in the rain tonight. Can I stay here?" I looked at this man, and without hesitation, I told him that he could stay. He has not left my side since.

Many times I talked to him and asked him what gave him the peace that had sustained him through all of his hard times. His answer was always, "I trust God." I brought him into my home, and I heard him worshiping God. He never complained, and he was quick to lend a helping hand. I believe he was sent to teach me. I am grateful for the lesson and the wisdom he has imparted. My dear old friend has since passed.

My friends, can you imagine trusting God while not having anything? Trusting and believing that He alone would provide for you? All the while still having a joyful smile on your face? For me, in my times of despair, I try to keep my eyes on Jesus.

Matthew 14:30 (NIV) summarizes the Christian life. "But when he saw the wind, he was afraid and, beginning to sink, cried out, 'Lord, save me!'" There is no secret to living the Christian life. The Bible clearly teaches that as we live by faith, in the same way we are saved by grace through faith in the Lord Jesus Christ.

An example of incredible faith is demonstrated in the life of Peter, one of Jesus's disciples. Peter obeyed the Lord and had the faith and courage to literally get out of a perfectly good boat and walk on water. That took a tremendous amount of faith. He was able to continue to walk on the water without sinking until the minute he took his eyes off Jesus and began to focus on the rushing winds on the stormy Sea of Galilee. As his faith waned, he began to sink and cried out in desperation, "Lord save me!"

Children of God, it's not mere coincidence that the scripture presents this incredible event in order to inspire us. God wants every Christian to learn the importance and the immense possibilities when we keep our mind and heart focused upon the Lord Jesus Christ. The story of Peter walking on water, sinking, and then crying out to the Lord to be saved is a beautiful truth that even a young child can comprehend. We must all keep unwavering eyes on Jesus!

The world cannot accept Him because it neither sees Him nor knows Him. But you know Him, for He lives with you and will be in you. "I will not leave you as orphans; I will come to you. Before long, the world will not see Me anymore, but you will see Me. Because I live, you also will live. On that day, you will realize that I am in My Father, and you are in Me, and I am in you. Whoever has My commands and keeps them is the one who loves Me. The one who loves Me will be loved by My Father, and I too will love them and show Myself to them." (John 14:18-24). These are the very words of our Father. He clearly states and urges us to keep His commandments. He is not asking us to be perfect but to simply obey.

Therefore, if Jesus lives within you, He will give you the peace that surpasses all understanding because you know He will take care of your every need. We can all take a valuable lesson from my homeless friend, who had a sense of peace in knowing that God would provide for him. The peace He exudes affects all around him. Somethings are beyond our control. We never know what situation we will find ourselves in. Consider one another with love and compassion.

In Colossians 3:15 (NIV), Paul wrote, "Let the peace of Christ rule in your hearts, since as members of one body you were called to peace. And be thankful."

Hebrews 12:14 (NIV) says, "Make every effort to live in peace with everyone and to be holy; without holiness no one will see the Lord."

In 1 Peter 5:7 (NIV), the Bible instructs us, "Cast all your anxiety on Him because He cares for you." Do not take for granted anything. The things of this world means nothing. Carry God in your heart and be pure.

James 3:18 (NIV) says, "Peacemakers who sow in peace reap a harvest of righteousness."

Dear Jesus,

Give me the peace and reassurance that you are with me at

all times. I will sound the shofar and announce to the evil one that Jesus Christ of Nazareth has defeated him. His plans are null and void against me, my family, my friends, and the nation. In Jesus's name. Amen.

Make a List of Things That Brings You Peace

_____

_____

_____

_____

_____

_____

_____

_____

_____

_____

_____

_____

HEALTH TIP #10: **Consume Probiotics**

Scientists are learning more each day about the important digestive role of microbes in keeping people healthy and the multitude of health benefits associated with consuming the right type and levels of probiotic microbes. Research has suggested that probiotic bacteria can

1. improve bodily functions;
2. reduce diarrhea associated with antibiotic therapy;
3. help reduce the risk of certain acute common infectious diseases; and
4. improve tolerance to lactose and much more.

So if I were you I would take two capsules nightly.

DAY 11

MY GOD, MY GOD, WHERE ARE YOU?

Because I have direct contact with my community and many trust me as a friend, people have confided their troubles to me. What saddens my heart greatly are the constant stories of suicide and drug overdose in the county I live in. This one story particular stood out to me the most: a young woman recently overdosed and not only was it an untimely and tragic death but also this young lady's mother had fallen into the same trap about a year before. Not to mention her father had committed suicide while in jail; an entire family gone too soon.

It breaks my heart to know that this young lady had no one to turn to, no one who would give a loving word of concern, and that she had turned to the streets and become addicted to drugs. There are countless other young people that I hear of who are also committing suicide. There are people we encounter every day that are in extreme circumstances, their pain is real and palpable. We must be sensitive to their needs and try to provide comfort and inspiration to them in their darker times.

People of God, we do not serve a God who does not understand our pain. This brings to mind the scripture verse where Jesus Himself cried out. "About three in the afternoon Jesus cried out in a loud voice, "Eli, Eli, lema sabachthani?" (which means, "My God, my God, why have you forsaken me?)" (Matthew 27:46 NIV) Here we see that even Jesus felt deep agony, but He cried to His father for strength. There is certainly a lesson here for us all. The Bible says we are our brothers' keepers.

I run a support group where I minister to people. This is my way to give back to my community and help those who feel like they are stuck. The beautiful thing about doing such work is the love and gratitude you get in return. All lives matter to Jesus.

Since I firmly believe that healing is spiritual, physical, mental, and emotional, we must address all four areas before we can become whole. I have witnessed many people getting well from major illnesses by freeing themselves of the lies they have held onto for years. Most importantly, they are being taught to forgive those who have wounded them. Guilt and shame do not have any place in the kingdom of God. Time to be free.

Forgiveness is the key to healing. Although I have helped many people in this group, the ministry has also helped me heal from the pain that I have carried since childhood. I thank God for the transparency we show each other during our sessions. It's definitely a time to be real. Go to God with your pain and struggles. Find a support group that is based on the word of God. Pray together.

In Psalm 25:5 (NIV), David prayed, asking God, "Guide me in your truth and teach me, for you are God my Savior, and my hope is in You all day long."

Shakti Gawain, a well-known author, most astutely said, "Evil (ignorance) is like a shadow—it has no real substance of its own, it is simply a lack of light. You cannot cause a shadow to disappear by trying to fight it, stamp on it, by railing against it, or any other form of emotional or physical resistance. In order to cause a shadow to disappear, you must shine light on it."

As human beings, we find ourselves crying out, but I assure you that Jesus is always with you.

Some may be feeling as if God is far from you, and you ask just as David did, "Why are you so far from saving me, so far from my cries of anguish? My God, I cry out by day, but you do not answer. I cry by night, but yet I find no rest. Yet you are enthroned as the Holy One; You are the one Israel praises. In You, our ancestors put their trust; they trusted and You delivered them. To You they cried out and were saved; in You they trusted and were not put to shame." Here we see that David cried to God in anguish, but as you continue to read on in the book of Psalms, there are many prayers of victory. God will never leave you.

I urge you to reach out to people who are in need. You will find that your burdens will become lighter. Lend a helping hand. Mentor. Do whatever you can; each one of us can make a difference. We are living in the cruelest of times, and our young people are dying because they feel that God has forsaken them. Each and every one of us can do something to help one another, however little it might be, even if it's just a smile. Go the extra mile to show that you care.

We are God's hands and feet on the earth, so it is our job to make those around us know, understand, and feel God's love. Though at times we ourselves may feel cast aside by God, if we really look around us, we will see God through the people we have encountered. And through helping others we will help ourselves.

Can you imagine what Jesus was thinking before He died? "Those who passed by hurled insults at him, shaking their heads and saying, 'You who are going to destroy the temple and build it in three days, save Yourself! Come down from the cross, if You are the Son of God!' In the same way, the chief priests, the teachers of the law, and the elders mocked Him. 'He saved others,' they said, 'but He can't save Himself! He's the king of Israel! Let Him come down now from the cross, and we will believe in Him. He trusts in God. Let God rescue Him now if He wants Him, for He said, 'I am the Son of God.' In the same way, the criminals who were crucified with Him also heaped insults on Him." (Mark 15:29-32 NIV)

Right before Jesus died, He understandably felt forsaken and abandoned. The onlookers mocked Him and His Father. He was bloody and broken, hanging on a cross, facing a slow and agonizing death for all to see. But yet He did not forsake His belief, and He prayed for the two thieves beside Him, giving them not only a kind word but eternal life. How powerful is this?

For those who may feel like your life is over, and thoughts of suicide linger because you feel as if you've failed, perhaps you believe the negative words that were spoken to you, sometimes even words spoken against you, that is driving you to your mortal limits, I pray that the power of Christ the King give you joy now!

Pray that God heal you so that You can become the driving force that gives humanity a semblance of hope, no matter how small. Lord, even before your death you had love, compassion, and forgiveness. Help us to be more like you. In Jesus's name. Amen.

In Remembrance of What Jesus Did Before
He Died, Even When He Felt Forsaken
by God, Can You Think of Ways You Can
Reach Out and Make a Difference?

_____

_____

_____

_____

_____

_____

_____

_____

_____

_____

HEALTH TIP #11: **Relieving Abdominal/Stomach Pain**

Abdominal/stomach pains can be felt anywhere from below your ribs to your pelvis. Chronic pain in the abdomen can also be a sign of a serious illness. Consult your physician if the pain persists.

- Lemon is a natural remedy for stomachache. Found at most grocery stores, lemon tea, when mixed with honey, can soothe the stomach.
- Ginger tea will also bring relief of stomach pain. Ginger tea can be bought in tea bags or made from its powdered form.
- Baking soda restores the pH balance in the body and prevents infections, this will relieve the pain and bloating. It's best taken by half a tablespoon mixed in half a cup of water.
- Eat yogurt if you are suffering from indigestion. This can be a reason for abdominal pain. Plain yogurt works best for me.

DAY 12

GOD'S TIMING NOT OURS

As humans, our natural instinct is a right-now attitude. We want an answer or a result instantly. Waiting on God's timings (and not ours) can be super stressful. You may become weary, but we must not be faint of spirit! I myself battle with this right now attitude.

So many times I have become impatient with God and have expected an immediate and positive answer. Perhaps it was a concern, or I was seeking an answer on finance or a question on the quality of a relationship. Maybe it was a request for the needs for my children. We all can relate to this desire at one time or another.

God will not answer you at the time you want Him to. However, I can promise you that He is an on-time God, operating on His own schedule. I believe through the waiting He wants us to worship Him. Be thankful and believe. His desire is for us to have patience in knowing that, whether good or bad, we will be okay.

Joyce Meyers said in her writing, "The tendency to want to know about everything that's going on can be detrimental to your Christian walk." But, you say, knowing would help carry me through this graveyard. Knowing would help me stop crying. You say things are getting worst, and God is silent. God gives us just enough. Imagine if we had a heads up of what's to come? Wouldn't that overwhelm us?

I spent a large part of my life being impatient, frustrated, and disappointed because I wanted to know what was going on. I needed to know what's happening next, or I wanted to know who my husband would be. I wanted God to give me a glimpse of him in a dream. I went on and on, constantly asking about everything. God had to teach me to leave things alone and quit wanting to know everything. I finally learned to trust the One who knows all things and accept that some questions will be answered in their own time. We must exercise our faith and prove that we trust God by refusing to worry. How many of us can relate?

Psalm 27:14 (NIV) instructs us, "Wait for the Lord; be strong and take heart and wait for the Lord."

In Proverbs 3:5–6 9 (NIV), the Bible says, "Trust in the Lord with all your heart and lean not on your own understanding; in all your ways submit to him, and he will make your paths straight."

Lamentations 3:25–26 (NIV) states, "The Lord is good to those whose hope is in Him, to the one who seeks Him; it is good to wait quietly for the salvation of the Lord." David prayed and cried out to the Lord saying, "My times are in Your hands; deliver me from the hands of my enemies, from those who pursue me."

My friends, even though we are impatient, I urge you to strengthen your faith by seeking an understanding of God's promise to us. His timing may not be ours, but I can assure you, He knows what's best for us. The Lord, is patient, kind and hopeful and time is in His hands. Trust Him!

God's timing is never early, and it's never late. God will accomplish His divine purpose in our lives on His schedule and not ours. Don't rush anything. When the time is right, it will happen; you being upset will not speed up or change a thing.

Stacey Charter once stated, "Life is all about timing ... The unreachable becomes reachable, the unavailable become available, the unattainable ... attainable. Have the patience, wait it out. It's all about timing."

My God, what a powerful insight! Think about this for a moment.

Have you ever wanted something so badly that you literally chased it down—hunted it down—I mean, did whatever you could, only to be disappointed when you did not receive it? Then, when you finally gave up and placed it in God's hands, it came at a later time? Perhaps you were not ready to receive such a gift at the time. God always knows best! Ask God for the lesson in the waiting.

God knew us before we were born, so therefore He knows everything we would encounter. He is not a puppet for us, and we cannot rush Him.

David Wilkerson said, "Never in the history of mankind has God taken anything from one of His children without bringing in something better, more beautiful, more fulfilling." Rest in God's peace, believing with confidence that His timing for your life is perfect. Ask God for peace and rest while you wait for his response.

Lord, help me to wait patiently for what you have for me. Give me faith and endurance to run the race of a life with you. Your timing is perfect. Help me while I wait upon you. In Jesus's name. Amen.

What Have You Been Praying for? Write a
Written Request and Place It into Your Bible.

_____

_____

_____

_____

_____

_____

_____

_____

_____

_____

_____

_____

HEALTH TIP #12: **The Benefits of Climbing Stairs**

If possible, you should choose to take the stairs instead of using the elevator. Climbing stairs strengthens the leg muscles and provides an excellent cardiovascular workout at the same time. This can be done at home, in your office, apartment building, or stair-climbing machines at the gym.

Don't overdo it when you begin, and you will find that, over time, you will be able to climb more steps at a little faster pace.

Move the body!

DAY 13

GOD'S PLAN IS BIGGER THAN YOURS

When I was around the age of fourteen or fifteen, I wanted to be a nun. My admiration for Mother Teresa was so great that I set my heart on this, but my life ultimately took a different direction—not the one I had planned, but quite the opposite. Nevertheless, though I could not have realized it at the time, God's plan was greater and better than mine.

Today, although my desire to emulate Mother Teresa through the religious order did not occur, I still serve God's people, God uses me as an instrument for ministering and healing, and I am most grateful.

I must say that, had it not been for all the things I have gone through, I would have never been able to relate to God's people like I do today. And just like Mother Teresa, I feel the strong calling to minister and love God's people.

In my humble prayers to God, I now pray his will for me daily. I still feel this hunger deep within, and God knows my desire and love for him. Mother Teresa took on the mission of proclaiming God's thirsting love for humanity, especially for the poorest of the poor. With such passion for God, we know that her desire and pursuit for God and His people was the gift that God placed in her. I am sure that at one point or another she had other plans for her life, but God's plans had her destined to be known to the world as a humanitarian.

Proverbs 16:9 (NIV) states, "In their hearts, humans plan their course, but the Lord establishes their steps." Sometimes God will have you doing things you never imagine doing.

In Romans 12:2 (NIV), the Bible says, "Do not conform to the pattern of this world, but be transformed by the renewing of your mind. Then you will be able to test and approve what God's will is—his good, pleasing and perfect will."

The Bible further states in Psalm 32:8 (NIV), "I will instruct you and teach you in the way you should go; I will counsel you with my loving eye on you."

How powerful is this? My friends, this alone should encourage us to fight the good fight of faith in Jesus and trust that His plan is bigger than ours.

I urge you to silence yourself before almighty God and allow Him to guide you into His perfect plan for your life.

I don't know about you, but I certainly want God to complete what He has started in me and write His love letter through my life. When we pray for guidance, we must believe He will put us where He wants us to be. He speaks and instructs us in his word.

Romans 1:9–11 (NIV) says, "God, whom I serve in my spirit in preaching the gospel of His Son, is my witness how constantly I remember You in my prayers at all times; and I pray that now at last by God's will, the way may be opened for me to come to You. I long to see You so that I may impart to you some spiritual gift to make you strong."

Heavenly Father, pour into me the spiritual gift you

predestined me for. Prepare me to be the end time warrior that is mighty in tearing down strongholds. Send me. Choose me. I am a willing vessel. My hopes, dreams, and desires are at your feet. I surrender to you, in Jesus's name. Amen.

Think of a Time You Had a Plan for Yourself
but God Had Something Else in Mind.

_____

_____

_____

_____

_____

_____

_____

_____

_____

_____

_____

_____

HEALTH TIP #13: **Anxiety**

Anxiety can be caused by depression, disturbed sleep, nutritional deficiencies, nicotine, adrenal disorders, thyroid disorders, and certain medications.

- Chamomile tea or the herbal supplement can help ease anxiety.
- The fresh smell of oranges and orange peels helps calm the nerves. They also help fight depression and boost immunity.
    1. Peel an orange and inhale the aroma
    2. Boil the orange peel and let the aroma refresh the home
- Nutmeg fights depression and promotes relaxation. One of the best ways to feel the benefits would be to use the essential oil. One-quarter teaspoon of nutmeg powder in food also has been shown to have benefits.
- The product Nutri-Calm, by Nature's Sunshine, is a product that can help with anxiety. Take as prescribed or on the advice of your health-care professional

DAY 14

LET GO AND LET GOD!

Years ago, God gave me the idea to create a group that would teach people about alternative health. At this time, many people were falling sick with cancer and other ailments, and they were telling me about the medicines they were taking that were not helping but making them feel worse. I stayed away from the idea of the healing group because, during the day, I spent so much time helping people nutritionally that by day's end I was drained, it seemed it would be too much for me.

Nevertheless, I continued working long hours, six days a week in my health food store, giving my service and advice free as many people could not afford to pay. As a result, I had let go of the idea of having the group.

One day a customer walked into my store and told me, "Doc, what you do here is so valuable that we need you to have a class once a week to teach people." It absolutely amazed me, because this was exactly what God had told me to do. Still I hardened my heart against it.

I had convinced myself that the task would be too much for me. She offered to start the meetings as long as I was present, and I agreed. The woman figured out the times and dates the group would meet, gathered the people, and started the group. It was her group, so the burden was not on my shoulders.

After the first meeting, she left, never to return. People were gathering weekly. I had no choice but to continue on after seeing how positive the outcome was. Today, looking back, I know that God sent her to get me started. Little did I know that my ministry, Silent Cry, Loud Echo, would be birthed from this one little group meeting.

God told me that His people were silently crying out, but their cries had created a loud echo in heaven and God had heard their cry. I needed to be obedient and allow God to use me the way He saw fit.

For three years, the group has continued meeting, and the number of people in attendance has steadily grown. We noticed that in order for people to heal themselves physically, emotionally, and spiritually, they needed to be transparent in all aspect of their lives. Some people hid sexual abuse, rape, and verbal abuse, and in group, they were able to speak of it for the very first time. This was healing in itself. We invited people from every walk of life to join us to heal and grow. God began to do great things. I witnessed cancer turnaround and major illnesses.

There was a need to expand and reach out to the community even more, so we added intercessory prayer on Tuesday nights, where we pray for guidance and instruction on where to go next. Because of the high suicide rate we were hearing about, Monday nights are reserved for the youth ministry where we mentor young people on how to make positive changes for not only themselves, but also their community.

People of God, I'm saying all this to tell you that we cannot resist nor fight God's plan. It's best to let go and allow Him to take charge. Remember that God will never leave you alone—He will always send you people who are like-minded to reach out and help you.

For me, if I can impact one life through my efforts, I know it's worth it. God allowed me to expand into my community with my ministry. It all started with this one woman who came in with the idea of a group meeting which evolved into writing books.

I love a quote by Mahatma Gandhi: "A small body of determined spirits fired by an unquenchable faith in their mission can alter the course of history."

I pray that you find the courage to go where God is calling you. As for me, I've decided to let go and let God.

> God, I'm giving up control, because you can control
> the things that are out of control in my life.
> —Pastor Rick Warren

In Romans 8:28 (NIV), He says, "And we know that in all things God works for the good of those who love Him, who have been called according to His purpose."

Psalm 46:10 (NIV) states, "He says, 'Be still, and know that I am God; I will be exalted among the nations, I will be exalted in the earth.'"

Minister Joyce Meyer said, "I believe that a trusting attitude and a patient attitude go hand in hand. You see, when you let go and learn to trust God, it releases joy in your life. And when you trust God, you're able to be more patient. Patience is not just about waiting for something … It's about how you wait, or your attitude while waiting."

What Is It You Need to Let Go Of and Let God Handle?

_____

_____

_____

_____

_____

_____

_____

_____

_____

_____

_____

_____

HEALTH TIP #14: **Backaches**

Backaches may result from many things: muscular tension, improper diet, lack of physical activity, arthritis, excessive physical labor, poor sedentary posture, pregnancy, and so on.

- Ginger is an anti-inflammatory and can be taken take as tea or an herbal supplement.
- Garlic oil massaged into back can alleviate back pain.
- Everflex, a product by Nature's Sunshine, can be used to get rid of muscular tension and this is very effective. I have seen it work on hundreds of people.
- Hot baths and stretching exercises have also been known to help. Eating a healthy diet is a must!

DAY 15

WHEN GOD SPEAKS, BLOCK OUT THE NAYSAYERS

When I decided to go forward with the Silent Cry, Loud Echo Ministry, not everyone believed that I could do it. There were genuine concerns from people close to me that I had already taken on too much and that the emotion of the ministry would wear me thin. Because I highly respected a few of them, I too began to doubt my ability.

Even though I did entertain this thought for a few moments, God did not allow me to stay in that mind-set. You see, when God tells you to do something, He will give you the confidence and the boldness to proceed. He will also put people in your path to support you in your endeavor.

Luke 9:1–2 (NIV) says, "When Jesus had called the Twelve together, He gave them power and authority to drive out all demons and to cure diseases, and He sent them out to proclaim the kingdom of God and to heal the sick."

In Mark 16:15 (NIV), the Bible explains, "He said to them, 'Go into all the world and preach the gospel to all creation.'"

And Mark 16:20 (NIV) goes on, "Then the disciples went out and preached everywhere, and the Lord worked with them and confirmed His word by the signs that accompanied it."

In Exodus 4:10–12 (NIV), we learn, "Moses said to the Lord, 'Pardon your servant, Lord. I have never been eloquent, neither in the past nor since you have spoken to your servant. I am slow of speech and tongue.' The Lord said to him, 'Who gave human beings their mouths? Who makes them deaf or mute? Who gives them sight or makes them blind? Is it not I, the Lord? Now go; I will help you speak and will teach you what to say.'" This is powerful indeed!

John 17:3 (NIV) states, "Now this is eternal life: that they know you, the only true God, and Jesus Christ, whom you have sent." This scripture clearly states that it is God's plan for us to know Him intimately. Therefore, we must learn to hear His voice so we know His will apart from our own.

God speaks to us in many ways, and He is not limited to one form of communication. In the scriptures, God spoke in various ways, including angels, His chosen spokesmen (prophets), dreams, visions, miracles, and even through a donkey that he enabled to speak as if a man.

In Romans 1:18–20 (NIV), Paul writes, "The wrath of God is being revealed from heaven against all the godlessness and wickedness of people, who suppress the truth by their wickedness, since what may be known about God is plain to them, because God has made it plain to them. For since the creation of the world, God's invisible qualities - His eternal power and divine nature - have been clearly seen, being understood from what has been made, so that people are without excuse."

In Psalm 19:1–2 (NIV), the Bible says, "The heavens declare the glory of God; the skies proclaim the work of His hands. Day after day, they pour forth speech; night after night they reveal knowledge."

Have confidence in what God is telling you and move forward. As for those who don't believe in you and your vision, don't pay them much mind. Keep your faith in Jesus and continue to seek Him.

Jesus will neither leave you nor forsake you. Remember: not everyone who starts with you will finish with you. When God is taking you to that next level, there's not going to be room for everyone on that journey.

Believe that when God speaks, and no matter how things might look, His word will never fail. In Isaiah 55:11 (NIV), the Lord spoke, "So in My word that goes from My mouth: It will not return to you void, but will accomplish what I desire and achieve the purpose for which I sent it." Here it is clear that He will accomplish that which He has started. For me, I am grateful that I have the opportunity to be used by almighty God.

Jesus has called each and every one of us to an assignment and a personalized mission for Him. We must heed that calling! He is preparing His end of time, with warriors that will come with power and miracles just as He did when He walked the Earth.

Jesus said, "But make up your mind not to worry beforehand, how you will defend yourselves. For I will give you words and wisdom that none of your adversaries will be able to resist or contradict. You will be betrayed even by parents, brothers, sisters, relatives, and friends, and they will put some of you to death" (Luke 21:14–16 NIV). Be not discouraged, rise with power and strength in the name of Jesus!

Has Someone Discouraged Your Vision and Tried to Make You Stop? List Ways to Help You Move Forward

_____

_____

_____

_____

_____

_____

_____

_____

_____

_____

_____

_____

HEALTH TIP #15: **Alleviating Muscle Cramps**

Muscles cramps are usually caused by exercising, walking, or doing daily activities. Other reasons include dehydration or lack of minerals like calcium, potassium, or manganese.

- Add two cups of Epsom salts to a warm bath and soak for half an hour. I love to drop some lavender oil in my bath tub at all times.
- Mix a tablespoon of apple cider vinegar in a glass of warm water and drink it once daily; it helps to soothe and relax the body and helps with sore muscles.
- Adding a half cup of apple cider vinegar to bathwater helps soothe, detox, and relax the body.
- Massage clove oil into the affected area.
- Blackstrap molasses is a good source of vital minerals and vitamins, such as iron, calcium, magnesium, vitamin B6, and selenium. Ingest a tablespoon daily.

DAY 16

HIS EYE IS ON THE SPARROW AND I KNOW HE WATCHES ME

One of my favorite things to do is to spend quiet time with God, meditating and praying. Sometimes, when I close my eyes, I can picture God looking down on me in a powerful and most anointing way—his eyes, full of love and compassion, looking on me as if I was the only one in this world. Can you imagine that comfort? I believe God honors a one-on-one relationship with us. You see, He compares us to no one!

Our amazing Lord and Savior loves us so much that He gave His life for us. And aren't you glad that He has no favorite among us? In Job 34:19 (NIV), He said, "Who shows no partiality to princes and does not favor the rich over the poor, for they are all the work of his hands?."

He went on to say in Matthew 10:29–31 (NIV), "Are not two sparrows sold for a penny? Yet not one of them will fall to the ground outside your Father's care. And even the very hairs of your head are all numbered. So don't be afraid; you are worth more than many sparrows." Glory to his name!

Growing up, I regularly heard, "God provides for the birds in the air; how much more would He not provide for us?" Upon pondering this, I ask this question: "How can I be discouraged when I know His eyes are on the sparrow and I know He loves and cares for me?"

Civilla Martin, the author of the well-known song, "His Eye Is on the Sparrow," had gone to visit a friend who had fallen ill. During that visit, she was struck by an inspiration. "One day, while we were visiting with the Doolittles, my husband commented on their bright hopefulness and asked them for the secret of it. Mrs. Doolittle's reply was simple: 'His eye is on the sparrow, and I know he watches me.'"

The beauty of this simple expression of boundless faith fired the imagination of Dr. Martin and has also inspired me. The song "His Eye Is on the Sparrow" was the outcome of that experience.

Why should I feel discouraged, why should the shadows come,
Why should my heart be lonely, and long for heav'n and home,
When Jesus is my portion? My constant Friend is He:
His eye is on the sparrow, and I know He watches me!

Take comfort my beloved that He cares! So many times these most minor of birds are overlooked and disregarded. Little boys have been known to torment them, and adults complain about how quickly they multiply and consider them pests.

Jesus specifically used the analogy of the unappreciated sparrow to show us how much He cares for the least of His creatures! If God is concerned about the tiny sparrow, how much greater must His concern be for man, who is immeasurably greater in value than the sparrow? Be encouraged today, for God is on your side. Be bold!

"I have told you these things, so that in me you may have peace. In this world you will have trouble. But take heart! I have overcome the world," says John 16:33 (NIV).

"You are my hiding place; you will protect me from trouble and surround me with songs of deliverance. I will instruct you and teach you in the way you should go; I will counsel you with my loving eye on you," Psalm 32:7–8 (NIV) explains. His loving eyes are upon us. This makes me want to shout!

"The mind governed by the flesh is death, but the mind governed by the Spirit is life and peace." (Romans 8:6 NIV) Keep your eyes upon your master.

List Ways to Encourage Yourself and Improve Your Situation

HEALTH TIP #16: **Common Signs That the Liver Is Toxic**

According to Healthy Food House, seven signs that the liver is toxic are the following:

1. Chronic fatigue
2. Excessive perspiration
3. Sudden weight gain
4. Difficulty digesting fats
5. Skin acne
6. Chronic bad breath

Treatments that will help and that I have used in my practice include the following:

- Milk thistle—protects the liver; it can be found in capsule, liquid, or tea form.
- Turmeric—taken internally, prevents damage to liver.
- Globe artichoke—improves function of liver.

DAY 17

YOUR STORMS ARE PREPARATIONS FOR YOUR DESTINY

Think of a time in your life when you believed you were going through a horrific experience, a time when you thought that the pain would never end and that you would never be able to come out of it alive, where it seemed you were buffeted from all angles, encountering one misfortune after another. Perhaps you thought you would lose your mind, and it would disable you forever. You found yourself feeling as if the very life was being pulled out of your body, and then the worst thoughts entered your mind, filling you with despair, making you murmur out of your breath, "God, I just want to die!"

I too have been there, and it is comforting to know that Jesus knows our troubles and cares for us. I recall the times when I was stricken and tormented with grief and as a result found out that I had a seven-pound tumor. Restful sleep was rare; I shut myself away from the world, not wanting to see or be around anyone. It was then that God, in His sovereignty, would show up.

I remember reading an article where the author said that the storms of life are caused by Satan. While true, God often allows these troubles as a test to our faith and loyalty to Him.

Take our brother Job's life into consideration: Job had experienced three tragedies back to back, including the loss of all his children. As I consider Job's life, I must say that it gives me great admiration and respect for his incredible faith in God!

In Job 23:10 (NIV), even though God allowed all those tragedies (He is in charge), His word states, "But he knows the way that I take; when He has tested me, I will come forth as gold." His faith remained strong in Jesus in spite of all he had endured.

"In all this you greatly rejoice," Peter 1:6–9 (NIV) tells us, "though now for a little while you may have had to suffer grief in all kinds of trials. These have come so that the proven genuineness of your faith - of greater worth than gold, which perishes even though refined by fire - may result in praise, glory and honor when Jesus Christ is revealed. Though you have not seen Him, you love Him; and even though you do not see Him now, you believe in Him and are filled with an inexpressible and glorious joy, for you are receiving the end result of your faith, the salvation of your souls."

Here we see that God allows all these storms so that we can be strengthened in faith and confidence that He alone will rescue us.

During my trials, with tears in my eyes and almost to the point of desperation, I recall confiding in one of my mentors that I didn't think I would make it through my desert experience. The tumor had grown so large that it was literally crushing my internal organs and my blood was low to the point that I could have collapsed at any moment. I needed a blood transfusion.

He looked at me, placed his hands on my shoulders, and said, "This too shall pass!" At that moment I could not see it, but looking back I can definitely agree with him now. God is allowing your present storms in preparation for your future destiny.

Martyn Lloyd-Jones wrote, "It is very difficult to be humble if you are always successful, so God chastens us with failure at times in order to humble us."

God wants the glory; therefore, we must manifest characteristics of Jesus Himself. Consequently, He will allow us to go through the storms.

In 2 Corinthians 12:7–10 (NIV), Paul tells us, "Therefore, in order to keep me from becoming conceited, I was given a thorn in my flesh, a messenger of Satan, to torment me. Three times I pleaded with the Lord to take it away from me. But He said to me, 'My grace is sufficient for you, for My power is made perfect in weakness.' Therefore, I will boast all the more gladly about my weaknesses, so that Christ's power may rest on me. That is why, for Christ's sake, I delight in weaknesses, in insults, in hardships, in persecutions, in difficulties. For when I am weak, then I am strong."

Upon pondering life's journey, I've come to realize that storms are inevitable. We cannot avoid them, but a true believer knows how to endure the whirlwinds and turbulence with the help of Jesus.

Keep in mind, when trials come, only our Savior can bring us peace. Remember that our Redeemer lives! God never promised us easy paths; what He did promise was that we would overcome in Him. God said that if we build our lives on the right foundation, we will not only overcome but be victorious.

I encourage you today to trust in God and understand that God does not allow storms in the lives of His children to destroy them, but to strengthen them! God wants us to seek Him and find strength and courage in Him. He wants us to trust in Him and believe in His promise to us.

In his parable about the storms and builders, Jesus teaches us that there are only two possible foundations to build upon in preparing for the storms of life: the rock and the sand. Here we see that Jesus is referring to His word when He speaks of the rock. When we build our lives according to God's word, then we are assured of His promises. There can be no victory without a battle. Keep in mind that storms come to apply stress to our foundation. Are you rooted and grounded in the word? If you are not grounded, you cannot overcome.

George S. Patton once said, "Battle is the most magnificent competition in which a human being can indulge. It brings out all that is best; it removes all that is base. All men are afraid in battle. The coward is the one who lets his fear overcome his sense of duty. Duty is the essence of manhood."

Nelson Mandela wrote one simple, but greatly impactful sentence, "It always seems impossible until it's done."

God bless you in your storms, fight the good fight of faith, keep your eyes on the prize. God is sharpening you for an awesome outcome. The world needs to hear your testimony.

Upon Reflection, How Have Your Storms of Life Prepared You for Now?

Are you a better and stronger person as a result of your battle?

_____

_____

_____

_____

_____

_____

_____

_____

_____

_____

_____

HEALTH TIP #17: **Sugar Cravings**

Carbohydrate and sugar cravings are signs of sugar addiction. Some of the signs that you have too much sugar in the body include the following:

1. Lack of energy and feelings of fatigue. If you are constantly feeling tired, consider cutting out excess sugars. Look into switching out unhealthy snacks for fruits or healthy nuts like almonds, walnuts, or brazil nuts.
2. Repeat occurrences of flu and colds. Sugar weakens the immune system, which makes it difficult to fight off illnesses.
3. If you feel foggy in the brain after meals, this means you might have low blood sugar. Try to eat fruits as they are natural sources of sugar.

Some ways to stop sugar cravings are to splash your face with cold water, tap your pressure points that are connected to appetite and cravings, and jog in one place. Also, add lecithin to your diet.

DAY 18

THOUGH YOU MAY BE IN A STORM, YOU ARE NOT ALONE

When the storms of life are like a raging wildfire, and you feel as if you are caught up in a flaming furnace, realize that you are not alone. God wants us to encourage each other to have faith and be still. He knows that we are facing much too much in these last days.

Understand that because God is sovereign, nothing can get through to you without first coming through Him. He is preparing you for greatness. The more we endure and become triumphant, the wiser we become. I believe this is why the Bible says to let the older women teach the younger ones in the Church.

Psalm 91:3–8 (NIV) says, "Surely He will save you from the fowler's snare and from the deadly pestilence. He will cover you with His feathers, and under His wings you will find refuge; His faithfulness will be your shield and rampart. You will not fear the terror of night, nor the arrow that flies by day, nor the pestilence that stalks in the darkness, nor the plague that destroys at midday. A thousand may fall at your side, ten thousand at your right hand, but it will not come near you. You will only observe with your eyes and see the punishment of the wicked."

Here God clearly affirms that He is there with us through it all.

Although I have been in situations in my life that seemed designed to break me, I was never alone. God always sent someone to be in my corner—He has even sent angels to comfort me. God has also given me dreams and visions to deliver comfort and tell me that everything would be fine. So even in the midst of great turmoil, I am comforted in knowing that it is not the end. He will do the same for you.

In the midst of unspeakable sorrow, God is with you even if you do not feel near Him. He has promised to never leave or forsake us. Jesus offers Himself to us as a shelter so that we can weather the storms of life under His gigantic wings and through His loving protection.

In John 14:18 (NIV), Jesus said, "I will not leave you as orphans; I will come to you." Here we see that even in the midst of that raging storm, we know that we are not alone. The Lord comes to minister peace to our hearts. God is present at all times.

I recall reading a book that told the story of Robert Bruce of Scotland. At the time of the story, he was running from captors who wished to persecute him. Bruce had taken shelter in a small cave when a spider came along and spun an elaborate web over the opening. Those who pursued him searched high and low in hopes of finding him. When they finally came across the cave where he hid, they passed it by thinking that Bruce never could have gotten through without breaking the spider's web.

Bruce breathed this prayer, "O God, I thank thee in the tiny bowels of a spider you can place for me a shelter"

No one enjoys suffering, but in the hands of the almighty God, trials become tools to temper and strengthen us. He uses hardship to shape believers into the people He intends them to be.

In Ephesians 6:13 (NIV), the Bible tells us, "Therefore put on the full armor of God, so that when the day of evil comes, you may be able to stand your ground, and after you have done everything, to stand." Stand!

Ask God to Reveal His Abiding Presence in the Midst of Your Troubles

Can You Think of a Time when You Felt God's Presence in the Midst of Your Despair? Write Your Story as a Testimony.

_____

_____

_____

_____

_____

_____

_____

_____

_____

_____

_____

HEALTH TIP #18: **Eat Beet Roots**

There is much nutritional value in beets. They contain vitamins A, B6, C, magnesium, zinc, iodine, chlorine, calcium, flavonoids, sodium, betaine, and nitrites. They are also high in antioxidants.

Beet roots reduce allergies and keep the kidneys, liver, and gallbladder healthy.

Some benefits of adding beet roots to the diet include the following:

1. They lower blood pressure due to nitrites they contain. Beets generate more nitrous oxide in the blood and help to lower the pressure.
2. Treat anemia and low iron
3. Better blood flow
4. Detox liver
5. Better skin

There are many ways to prepare beets, but the way to take them is either eating them raw or juicing them.

DAY 19

TAKE A CHANCE: WALK ON WATER WITH JESUS

At many times in my Christian life, I found myself challenged on what to do regarding my business. At the time of this writing, I have been in business for more than eight years. Although it's a fulfilling business and I have helped countless adults, children, and even animals, I was consistently losing money. I depleted my entire personal savings to sustain the business, to the point where I was forced to live from paycheck to paycheck. Each month I arrived at a point where I was hoping and praying that God would come through for me, and that my bills could be paid on time. I was stressed, exhausted, and drained, worrying about my financial hardship—but God has never let me down. I've never missed a payment in spite of the austere business climate. Even through all this God was putting me through transition; I would end one career in order to embark upon another.

My friends, sometimes God puts us in these situations to test our faith. For me, it's a great place to be because I get to see God move in my life. And I know, without a shadow of a doubt, that I can depend on Him to sustain me. Sometimes in life it's not all about finances. Don't get me wrong: I know we need money. But sometimes winning souls and making a sacrifice for God's people is worth the anxiety and heartache.

In spite of my desperate times, I continued to hope and trust in God. When God calls on you to help His people, it's not always about money. People constantly asked, "Are you making money here?" I told them that I wasn't, but that I was winning souls for Jesus and helping my community.

Take Mahatma Gandhi for an example. Gandhi was a well-educated attorney who stood up and fought against injustice. Despite being brought up at a high level in a caste system that afforded him the chance to have the best opportunities financially and educationally and the ability to live a wealthy and lavish life, Gandhi decided to help those who were less fortunate. Subsequently, he himself lived in poverty. He was a man of no material wealth, but he was extremely rich in character and love for all people. They called him "Father" in India.

One of my favorite quotes of his is "Be the change you want to see in the world."

Mother Teresa was another person who devoted her life to helping God's people and rarely if ever saw her own financial gain. As a child, Mother Teresa grew up in financial extremis, yet her mother's teachings and beliefs helped fuel her and her family to carry on. She had a deep love and passion for taking care of God's people, giving extra care to those who lived in extreme poverty. Mother Teresa's main goal was to bring God's hope and love unto the many people she met.

"For whoever wants to save their life will lose it, but whoever loses their life for me will save it" (Luke 9:24 NIV).

"Boaz replied, 'I've been told all about what you have done

for your mother-in-law since the death of your husband—how you left your father and mother and your homeland and came to live with a people you did not know before'" (Ruth 2:11 NIV). Glory to God! This scripture clearly tells us that our good works do not go in vain.

"By faith, Moses, when he had grown up, refused to be known as the son of Pharaoh's daughter. He chose to be mistreated along with the people of God rather than to enjoy the fleeting pleasures of sin. He regarded disgrace for the sake of Christ as of greater value than the treasures of Egypt, because he was looking ahead to his reward. By faith he left Egypt, not fearing the king's anger; he persevered because he saw him who is invisible." (Hebrew 11:24-27)

"Jesus answered, 'If you want to be perfect, go, sell your possessions and give to the poor, and you will have treasure in heaven. Then come, follow Me'" (Matthew 19:21 NIV). What position are you willing to give up for the sake of almighty God?

How much do you love Christ the king? Do you love Him more than your Earthly possessions? What if you were asked to give up everything? My beloved, I can honestly tell you that at one point in my life I lost everything, but the Lord never left me. I got a chance to see who He really is. He is indeed a faithful father. I urge you to prove Him for yourself. God will reward you in more ways than you can even fathom. Take a chance, walk on water with our beloved Father Yeshua the king.

What Are You Willing to Sacrifice in Order to Follow Jesus?

_____

_____

_____

_____

_____

_____

_____

_____

_____

_____

_____

HEALTH TIP #19: **Healthy Fruits**

Consumption of fresh fruits is very beneficial to our overall health and wellness. You should aim to eat between two and three servings of fruit each day. Some of the best ones and their benefits follow:

- Pineapple burns fat and tones the stomach and aids in digestions.
- Bananas have antiviral properties and prevents muscle cramps.
- Asian pears help remove free radicals and gives you vibrant skin.
- Oranges help sinus, respiratory issues and is great for the immunity.
- Currants help purify the blood and reduce anemia.
- Blueberries balance the blood and prevent hypertension.
- Apples prevent depression and anxiety and is a great form of fiber.
- Lime removes toxins from the body and aids in weight loss.
- Cherries strengthen the heart and circulatory system.

DAY 20

WHAT YOU BELIEVE DETERMINES WHAT YOU BECOME

C. S. Lewis once said, "Pain insists upon being attended to. God whispers to us in our pleasures, speaks in our consciences, but shouts in our pains. It is His megaphone to rouse a deaf world." We are a direct reflection of all our experiences and the beliefs we have formed while growing up. I firmly believe that what we become is a result of what we believe.

During the very worst of my situations, and at the times when I often felt that I had reached my limit, I refused to allow my belief system to change and become engulfed with the situation. I've firmly maintained that God would deliver me and that through His protection, the situation would soon pass. Napoleon Hill once said, "Whatever the mind can conceive and believe, it can achieve."

My friends, regardless of your current conditions, do not allow the essence of what you are to mutate in response to your trials and challenges. Remain steadfast in purpose and maintain the focus of your core being.

I have a friend who told me a story about himself that is the epitome of growth and the triumph of the mind over matter. This story will touch your life.

My friend was unfortunately undergoing multiple, serious life crises in a very short period of time. He lost both his parents within a seven-week period, and soon after that, he lost his own daughter. He became separated from his wife of many years and depleted his personal savings in trying to keep their business afloat. These circumstances, and the inherent stress and pain, caused him to begin drinking heavily and engage in inappropriate relationships with other women. He allowed his personal appearance to degrade, became angry and depressed, lost a lot of weight, and seemed on the edge of a nervous breakdown.

I believe that at this point God stepped in and caused my friend to realize what He had in mind for my friend to be. Through the word of God, he gained strength to overcome such devastation.

In a stroke of miracle, my friend found a picture of himself at age three, taken by his father. His father had taken the picture and had personally colored the photo on a canvas medium. The photo clearly captured the innocence and promise of the child.

His father was not a professional photographer—he had been seriously injured in the Second World War, and the army had trained him in photography as part of his extensive rehabilitation. In spite of the disabling injuries, his father had devoted the time and energies to produce a work of art.

When my friend found the picture, it jolted him and caused him to realize what he really was truly supposed to be, and what he truly was—not the near-alcoholic and depressed womanizer he was on a path to become.

My friend placed the picture in a prominent place in his home and looked at the picture often, reminding himself that he was truly a grown-up version of the kind, innocent little boy—not angry and depressed and on a trip to personal destruction.

He still displays the picture prominently on his fireplace mantle—he has curtailed the destructive behaviors that had plagued him during his time of distress. He now has normal, healthy relationships with women and has abandoned the excessive drinking and the anger he had. He is trying to forgive past wrongs, and I believe he is on the right path to heal the hurts of the past.

Belief has everything to do with your purpose! In Genesis 15:6 (NIV), the Bible explains, "Abram believed the Lord, and he credited it to him as righteousness." And in the New Testament, the apostle Paul said, "I can do all things through Christ who strengthens me."

Because I believe that Jesus has a plan for me, I have been able to think myself out of the worst situations. When you are confident in your God, He will deliver you and open unexpected doors beyond your wildest imagination. Speak to the negative things in your life; speak life into a bad situation.

You must believe the report of the Lord, as your past does not define who you will become. I was born into poverty in the third world country of Guyana. No one around me dreamed of a future beyond what was told to us; girls had to find a good husband and serve him, and boys had to take on responsibility of supporting a family at a young age.

In spite of the conditioning, I dreamed of the American

life: a good education, nice home, good job, freedom, and the possibility of growth in all aspects of my life. When I told my schoolmates that I dreamed of going to America, they literally laughed at me! I did not let that discourage me; instead, I continued to dream big! My father used to tell me all the time, "Do not let the confines of being in a third world country limit you to dream beyond the borders of Guyana." I dare you to dream beyond the borders of your situation.

Let what you believe become your vision for empowerment. Don't allow your negative issues and thoughts to prevent you from living a faithful and fulfilled life. God has a higher purpose for you—allow Jesus to change your story like He did for me and my friend.

In Matthew 9:28–29 (NIV), scriptures says, "And when He had come into the house, the blind men came to Him. And Jesus said to them, 'Do you believe that I am able to do this?' They said to Him, 'Yes, Lord.' Then He touched their eyes, saying, 'According to your faith, let it be to you'." And the blind were able to see again! I don't know about you, but I am excited about the works of almighty God.

In Isaiah 43:10 (NIV), "'You are My witnesses,' says the Lord, 'And My servant whom I have chosen, that you may know and believe Me, and understand that I am He. Before Me there was no God formed, nor shall there be after Me.'"

How powerful is this? Knowing that we serve a God that is all-powerful, He is able to change your circumstances and give you renewed Hope! I challenge you to believe in God's promise and watch Him blow your mind.9

John 6:35 (NIV) says, "And Jesus said to them, 'I am the

bread of life. He who comes to Me shall never hunger, and he who believes in Me shall never thirst.'" Dare to believe!

> Keep your dreams alive. Understand to achieve
> anything requires faith and belief in yourself, vision,
> hard work, determination, and dedication. Remember
> all things are possible for those who believe.
> —Gail Devers

We have always held to the hope, the belief, the conviction that there is a better life, a better world, beyond the horizon.
—Franklin D. Roosevelt

What is Standing Against the Belief that You Were Destined to do Great Things?

Stop believing the lies you were programmed with and retrain your belief system.

_____

_____

_____

_____

_____

_____

_____

_____

_____

_____

HEALTH TIP #20: **Consume Aloe Internally and Keep an Aloe Plant in Your House**

Aloe vera is a versatile plant with a wide array of medicinal properties. Due to this, it is known as the "wand of heaven." I have recommended this plant to numerous clients.

Topically, it can be used in the treatment of minor wounds, scrapes, cuts, and burns. When taken internally, in the form of capsules or liquid, this amazing plant provides even more health benefits such as

1. amino acids;
2. minerals; and
3. enzymes.

Aloe also effectively cleanses the body and helps to remove toxins. It is used by the digestive tract and relieves joint inflammation and much more. See a health care professional for further advice.

DAY 21

IF YOU KNOW WHO YOU ARE, THEN YOU KNOW WHO YOU ARE NOT

I was born in Guyana, South America, lived a humble life, and came to America when I was almost fifteen. The culture and climate of America were all so very different, and it was necessary for me to make large adjustments. I was very naive and trusted everyone.

I had a father back in Guyana who inspired me. I could recall as a child that he told me every day how beautiful I was and that I could do anything I put my mind to. He showered me with his love and affection.

But in spite of this exhortation, by the time I was introduced to my new environment I realized that I would not be so readily accepted. I was teased, called names, and ridiculed for the way I dressed. When I started high school, I did not have much clothing and wore the same attire a few times a week. Classmates didn't want to sit next to me. But through all the pain, the kind and empowering words my father instilled in me kept me afloat.

You see, if you know who you are, then you know who you are not! I don't care what people think and say to you, you do not have to believe them. No matter how you sometimes look and feel, never forget who you really are. You are made in God's image.

In 1 Peter 2:9 (NIV), the New Testament tell us, "But you are a chosen people, a royal priesthood, a holy nation, God's special possession, that you may declare the praises of Him who called you out of darkness into His wonderful light." Empower your mind with the word of God. Believe Jesus today!

In John 5:24 (NIV), Jesus said, "Very truly I tell you, whoever hears My word and believes Him who sent me has eternal life and will not be judged but has crossed over from death to life."

In 1 Peter 1:4 (NIV), the Bible says, "And into an inheritance that can never perish, spoil or fade. This inheritance is kept in heaven for you."

Psalm 125:1 (NIV)states, "Those who trust in the Lord are like Mount Zion, which cannot be shaken but endures forever."

We must be careful to what we listen to and guard our hearts against the corrupting influences that are everywhere in this world today. Be careful to discern the subtle voices that are constantly presenting seemingly appealing ideologies, which are, in fact, opposed to God. We must be wise and be quick to discern good from evil.

As Christians we are set apart! Therefore, we need to maintain balance. This can only be achieved when we put our entire life into God's hands. Always think positive, believe that God has a great plan for you. Do not believe the negative words of others. Do not allow ill treatment to cause you to turn bitter.

In whatever we do, we are doing as unto the Lord—with a grateful heart, not seeking anything but to please God. We will find our lives naturally aligning with God's perfect will and infused by His perfect peace.

A Chinese proverb says, "If there is light in the soul, there will be beauty in the person. If there is beauty in the person, there will be harmony in the house. If there is harmony in the house, there will be order in the nation. If there is order in the nation, there will be peace in the world." Encourage yourself, be determined that you will not do what has been done to you. Do you have a tendency to criticize others? I urge you to turn that attention to self-improvement. There must be harmony in all aspects of your life. Hunger for it.

Make a List of Your Strengths and Talents. Focus on Your Gifts.

_____

_____

_____

_____

_____

_____

_____

_____

_____

_____

_____

_____

HEALTH TIP #21: **Get Plenty of Fresh Air and Sunshine—It's Beneficial for Well-Being**

We can use everything at our disposal—he best foods, water, and plenty of exercise—but without fresh air and sunshine, we will not have total health.

Sunlight is a powerful healer, tonic, germ killer, remedial agent, and relaxer. When you spend time in the fresh air and sunlight, your body absorbs their life-giving elements. Scientists have discovered a strong connection between light and health. They have found that natural light has a very significant effect on our immune system and depression.

Fresh air and sunlight are life-giving. Without fresh air and sunlight, we, along with all forms of life, would die. Balance is the key. The rays of sun give energy and light, but too much of a good thing is destructive. Be careful and educate yourself on this matter. Sesame oil is a natural sunblock that I prefer and have recommended to my clients.

DAY 22

WHEN MAN REJECTS YOU, GOD IS WAITING WITH OPEN ARMS

Rejection is a very difficult thing to deal with, and for me, that is the area the devil has repeatedly used to torture me. It all started with my father. Not that he intentionally rejected me, but the feeling came about when I had to move from my country of birth to my new home here in the United States.

My father was my closest friend, my beloved, someone who I never doubted had my best interests in mind. After my move, I went from seeing my father daily to not being able to see him or even hear his voice for months on end. I received letters from him, but since my father was not much of a writer, they were few and far between. As the years went by and as we went back and forth with the letters, I determined that the one person I thought was on my team had abandoned me too. At that time, I even questioned God. I was lonely, sad, and scared. I believed my father could have come to the United States and be there for me, but he chose not to.

This quote written by an unknown author sums up my feelings at that time, "And maybe I pushed you away to see if you care enough to pull me back!" Because I felt so wounded, I pushed people away that said they loved me. Do you find yourself here?

An article I read in *Psychology Today* quoted, "When children are raised with chronic loss, without the psychological or physical protection they need and certainly deserve, it is most natural for them to internalize incredible fear. Not receiving the necessary psychological or physical protection equals abandonment. And, living with repeated abandonment experiences creates toxic shame. Shame arises from the painful message implied in abandonment: 'You are not important. You are not of value.'" (Understanding the Pain Of Abandonment. Claudia Black - www.psychologytoday.com/blog/the-many-faces-addiction)

This is the pain from which people need to heal. For some children, abandonment is primarily physical. Physical abandonment occurs when the physical conditions necessary for thriving have been replaced by lack of appropriate supervision, inadequate provision of nutrition and meals, inadequate clothing, housing, heat, or shelter, and physical or sexual (or both) abuse.

Today, many adults are living with secrets that manifest themselves in the form of illnesses. Unless we deal with the pain and hurt that have been swept under the rug, we cannot begin to recover and live the authentic life God intended for us.

The good news is that the Lord can heal you of all your infirmities. Only God can put a shattered glass back together just by one command. I am a witness to the healing power of God.

Deuteronomy 31:6 (NIV) says, "Be strong and courageous. Do not be afraid or terrified because of them, for the Lord your God goes with you; He will never leave you nor forsake you."

Romans 8:38–39 (NIV) explains, "For I am convinced that neither death nor life, neither angels nor demons, neither the present nor the future, nor any powers, neither height nor depth, nor anything else in all creation, will be able to separate us from the love of God that is in Christ Jesus our Lord."

Trust God and believe that He loves you, and remember that all things work together for good to those who trust in Him. In this life time, people will continually disappoint and abandon you. Perhaps it is your parents, your friends, etc. but I can assure you that God will never abandon you. Build your prayer life and pour your heart out to Jesus. He will help you to see the goodness of our God.

A book I recommend, *Love Me, Don't Leave Me* by Dr. Michelle Skeen, has one of my favorite quotes on abandonment: "When someone you loved finds no flattering in the gift you gave them, then you must ask yourself, 'What was worth loving?'"

As individuals, we all have experienced our own unique trauma that we have to deal with. I believe that when the abuse comes from a parent or from siblings, it is most difficult. This is why it is certainly impossible to prescribe a one-size-fits-all solution for the emotional processing that needs to occur in order for you to feel whole again. It is important to look for programs and methods that fit best for you and your recovery. I certainly recommend praying to Jesus for strength coupled with Christian counseling. Pray Psalm 23.

Questions to Ask Yourself

1. What are the strongholds in your life?
    Seek help. Be honest and transparent.

    _____

    _____

    _____

2. Are you a perfectionist? Do you tell yourself if
    only you get it right you won't be rejected?

    _____

    _____

    _____

3. When did this all start?

    _____

    _____

    _____

    _____

HEALTH TIP #22: Trying to Go Alkaline? Eat These Foods.

Alkaline foods are better for the body because they help to balance the pH that regulates overall body health. These eight foods help to alkalize the body.

1. Amaranth—grain with more protein than wheat and higher in the amino acid lysine than other grain sources of protein
2. Artichokes—highest antioxidant level of all vegetables
3. Arugula—leafy salad vegetable that contains high levels of protein, thiamin, riboflavin, vitamin B6, zinc, copper, and pantothenic acid (vitamin B5)
4. Asparagus—plenty of nutrients and is known as the antiaging vegetable
5. Avocado/avocado oil—high in potassium as well as healthy fat.
6. Basil—herb that helps the body heal
7. Broccoli—considered one of the world's healthiest foods

DAY 23

IF I GOT TOO COMFORTABLE, I WOULD HAVE STAYED: GOD ORCHESTRATED THE ENTIRE ORDEAL

In my life, I have learned that when I was able to step outside my safe place, I made the most progress. My friends, it is absolutely imperative that you step outside of your comfort zone and challenge yourself to do something you're not familiar with. The challenge will allow you to learn things about yourself you have not even discovered. You might even be amazed at the courage and faith that you possess to step over the high, raging waters that are facing you. I challenge you to explore possibilities beyond your imagination! Do not be afraid—God is with you.

So many times we find ourselves stuck in a situation that we know isn't right for us, but we stay anyway because we are afraid of the unknown!

In my private practice as a doctor of natural medicine, I come across people who tell me story after story of staying at a job they absolutely hate, being in a toxic relationship, and so on, and being forced to live in a constant survival mode of being unhappy and unable to sleep. They are mentally tortured with no proper nutrition, exercise, fresh air, or sunlight, but on and on, they go! No situational changes in sight, just the same old routine! How sad.

The common theme that I find in these people is that they complain of constant health issues. According to Dr. Nelson, "Your body is both biochemical and biophysical, and disruptions in your field of energy will eventually result in physical dysfunction. It's interesting to note that certain emotions are known to be associated with pain in certain regions of your body, even though science cannot give an explanation for why."

He went on to say, "For example, those suffering from depression will often experience chest pains, even when there's nothing physically wrong with their heart. Extreme grief can also have a devastating impact."

And, as noted in the film, *E-Motion*, the emotions associated with living in a "state of emergency" all the time—which is what happens when you're chronically stressed—are anger, aggression, hatred, fear, prejudice, anxiety, insecurity, hopelessness, and other negative states that feed the energetic chaos that manifests itself as physical pain and disease.

It is vitally important to recognize how carrying your destructive emotional baggage can adversely affect your health. You must change your way of thinking if you are to improve your condition. As for me, God is my healer and encourager! Use the word of God as food for your soul.

In an article written by Harold Herring, he listed "Seven Things You Must Do to Leave Your Comfort Zone." He then went on to say, "Your comfort zone is an enemy of your future. A hindrance to your success. A stumbling block to your destiny.

If you stay in your comfort zone, you will never leave nor surpass your current reality."

God says, in Joshua 1:9 (NIV), "Have I not commanded you? Be strong and courageous. Do not be afraid; do not be discouraged, for the Lord your God will be with you wherever you go."

And finally, my favorite, Proverbs 3:5–6 (NIV) says, "Trust in the Lord with all your heart and lean not on your own understanding; in all your ways submit to Him, and He will make your paths straight." Wow! He will make your crooked path straight. Take the chance and make the leap with Jesus, I promise you He will never disappoint you!

You would be surprised as you think about your life's journey, how much time and energy you spend worrying about things that never even happened and eventually turned for your good. Instead of worrying, channel that energy into something positive, seek God for complete guidance, and watch Him move and work on your behalf. Living under the cloud of what-ifs is not productive and will eventually destroy you.

In John 14:27 (NIV), Jesus says, "Peace I leave with you; My peace I give you. I do not give to you as the world gives. Do not let your hearts be troubled and do not be afraid." Oh, glory be to His holy name! Here we see our beloved Father encourages his children. My friends I don't know about you but this makes me want to shout!

All things you go through have been orchestrated by the Most High God and will ultimately work in your favor, so have a sense of peace when troubles arise. God sees all and He knows the solution.

Are You Afraid of Taking the Leap on a Decision
That Can Possibly Change Your Life? What's
the Negative Thoughts That Are Hindering You?
Replace Them with Ones That Are Positive

_____

_____

_____

_____

_____

_____

_____

_____

_____

_____

_____

HEALTH TIP #23: **Eat Plenty of Pineapple**

Pineapple has bromelain enzymes that kill pain and get rid of cough, making it a better option than cough medicine. It's full of B1, C, B2, B3, B5, and B6 vitamins as well as copper, magnesium, potassium, manganese, dietary fiber, folic acid, and beta carotene. Pineapple helps balance and neutralize fluids in the body by stimulating secretion of hormones in the pancreas. After each meal I like to eat a few pieces of pineapple. I keep this fruit in my refrigerator.

DAY 24

PASS THE TEST OF STAYING IN FAITH EVEN WHEN GOD IS SILENT

I heard a story related by a pastor I listen to very often. He told of a woman whose house went into foreclosure. She was devastated and had no means of saving her house. On the day of the foreclosure auction, the Holy Spirit led her to go witness the event. Even though she knew it would be painful to watch a total stranger purchase the house she had lived in for so many years, she wanted to see who the new owner would be. Upon entering the auction, she sat down close to a woman near the back of the room. As the auctioneer began, the woman next to her noticed her crying and asked why she was in tears. She answered and said, "The home you purchased was my home for many years." The woman was touched by the story and told her, "I was originally here to purchase a house for my son, but instead the Lord has prompted me to return it to you."

I believe that because she was obedient and stayed in faith, God allowed this stranger to bless her. She not only regained her home, but it was paid off! God restored what the enemy had taken, and blessed her for her troubles by paying off the home for her. In spite of the dire situation, God was working on her behalf. Be encouraged! Right before your biggest break through all Hell can break loose, be patient encourage yourself God is on the scene and ready to take action! Praise Him!

Jesus said, "Because you have so little faith. Truly I tell you, if you have faith as small as a mustard seed, you can say to this mountain, 'Move from here to there,' and it will move. Nothing will be impossible for you." (Matthew 17:20 NIV). Thus saith the Lord!

This brings me to the realization that your thoughts are important in spite of what your surroundings may look like. "Then Jesus said to the centurion, 'Go! Let it be done just as you believed it would.' And his servant was healed at that moment" (Matthew 8:13 NIV). "Everything is possible for one who believes." (Mark 9:23 NIV). Here God is saying that we must believe. Anything is possible.

Some may ask, "How is it, Lord, that I am living my life right, pleasing the Lord, and yet it still seems things are crumbling around me?" What do you do then? When you go to work daily, but still can't afford much because you are not making enough money? You feel that God is silent or that perhaps He is punishing you.

To whomever is feeling this way, I want you to pause for a moment and silence yourself, get on your knees, then fast, and pray. Do whatever it takes, seek God and submit your desires and wills to Him; allow Him to lead you and guide you. I heard someone once say, "The greater the challenge, the greater the victory."

Instead of moping and complaining, give thanks to God that you have not lost your mind. Hang tough and celebrate the fact that you are still alive. The devil would never try to slow you down if you were not a threat to him.

The present trials that you are going through are preparing you for the triumph that is to come. Joseph had to be rejected by his brothers, sold into slavery, accused by his boss's wife, thrown into prison, and forgotten by his cell mates in order for him to enter into the palace to become the number two man in Israel! He went from the pit to the palace.

You must stop crying and complaining, and start lifting your hands and begin to praise God for your breakthrough and your blessing. You cannot have the rewards before you go through the challenge. Remember: "...the one who is in you is greater than the one who is in the world." (1 John 4:44 NIV)

Believe God will help you do something supernaturally that you cannot do for yourself. Trust Him! Dance like David did.

Psalm 24 always encourages me. "The earth is the Lord's, and everything in it, the world, and all who live in it; for He founded it on the seas and established it on the waters. Who may ascend the mountain of the Lord? Who may stand in His holy place? The one who has clean hands and a pure heart, who does not trust in an idol or swear by a false god. They will receive blessing from the Lord and vindication from God their Savior. Such is the generation of those who seek Him, who seek Your face, God of Jacob. Lift up your heads, you gates; be lifted up, you ancient doors, that the King of glory may come in. Who is this King of glory? The Lord strong and mighty, the Lord mighty in battle. Lift up your heads, you gates; lift them up, you ancient doors, that the King of glory may come in. Who is he, this King of glory? The Lord Almighty—he is the King of glory."

Rejoice! God is at hand.

I love the quote by Eleonora Duse, "If the sight of the blue skies fills you with joy, if a blade of grass springing up in the fields has power to move you, if the simple things in nature have a message you understand, rejoice, for your soul is alive."

Unleash the power of thinking yourself out of your current situation. Make your plans and write them down—dream big!

Think about the Areas in Your Life Where
You Are Feeling Oppressed or Boxed In.
Allow God to Transform Them to a Praise.

_____

_____

_____

_____

_____

_____

_____

_____

_____

_____

_____

_____

HEALTH TIP #24: **Fast for Good Health**

Some of the health benefits of fasting are include the following:

1. Slows down the aging process and gives your organs a rest
2. Helps you beat addictions and is great for spiritual purposes
3. A great way to start a healthy diet and it clears your mind
4. Raises insulin sensitivity
5. Can normalize food cravings
6. Promotes the fat burning process
7. Clears the skin and whitens the eyes. It rids the body of toxins
8. Reduces cholesterol levels and high blood pressure
9. Regulates immune system cells and so much more

I suggest you do some research on your own before embarking upon this venture. I believe knowledge is powerful and a great eye opener.

DAY 25

GOD TOLD JOSHUA THAT MEDITATING ON HIS WORD WAS THE SECRET TO SUCCESS AND PROSPERITY

Meditating and memorizing the word of God gives you strength, courage, endurance, faith, and hope for a future; your very life depends on it. Along my path of life, I found that without the word of God, I felt unfulfilled and had no direction. Listening to the word of God strengthens your spirit, body, soul, and mind.

We must memorize God's written word as Jesus did so that when Satan comes at us with negative thoughts and lies, we can resist him and he will flee. In Joshua 1:8–9 (NIV), the Word clearly states to "keep this Book of the Law always on your lips; meditate on it day and night, so that you may be careful to do everything written in it. Then you will be prosperous and successful. Have I not commanded you? Be strong and courageous. Do not be afraid; do not be discouraged, for the Lord your God will be with you wherever you go."

Success and prosperity do not necessarily equate to money and wealth, but complete knowledge of God and His word is abundant wealth and great success. Without a plan and a direction, man will go astray. That is why we need to study the

Bible. It contains the mind of God and His will for each and every one of our lives. It is a road map, a guide for mankind.

In 2 Timothy 3:16–17 (NIV), the Bible says, "All Scripture is God-breathed and is useful for teaching, rebuking, correcting and training in righteousness, so that the servant of God may be thoroughly equipped for every good work."

Proverbs 30:5–6 (NIV) reveals, "Every word of God is flawless; He is a shield to those who take refuge in Him. Do not add to His words, or He will rebuke you and prove you a liar."

Psalm 119:89 (NIV) states, "Your word, Lord, is eternal; it stands firm in the heavens."

The Lord will speak to you through His scriptures—it is incumbent on you to listen and meditate upon His word. Isaiah 55:1 (NIV) says, "So is my word that goes out from my mouth: It will not return to Me empty, but will accomplish what I desire and achieve the purpose for which I sent it."

In Ephesians 6:1 (NIV), Paul instructs the believer to "put on the full armor of God, so that you can take your stand against the devil's schemes."

The answers to all of life's problems and challenges can be found in the Bible. God's word is a lamp to our feet and a light to our path. Meditating on the word will bring you wisdom.

In Proverbs 19:8 (NIV), the Bible explains, "The one who gets wisdom loves life; the one who cherishes understanding will soon prosper." We all have our seasons, it is imperative to be patient and continue to pray while we persevere in our endeavors.

We see that the word of God further explains itself in Proverbs 8:32–36 (NIV), "Now then, my children, listen to me; blessed are those who keep My ways. Listen to My instruction and be wise;

do not disregard it. Blessed are those who listen to Me, watching daily at My doors, waiting at My doorway. For those who find Me find life and receive favor from the Lord. But those who fail to find Me harm themselves; all who hate Me love death."

Proverbs 16:16 (NIV) is also very clear. "How much better to get wisdom than gold, to get insight rather than silver!"

This, my friends, is a matter of life and death. To live as a foolish man, just merely existing, is death. The ultimate eternal happiness can only be found by those who first "Seek after wisdom."

Proverbs 15:21 (NIV) says, "Folly brings joy to one who has no sense, but whoever has understanding keeps a straight course." Sadly, our thirst for happiness is insatiable in this world, and if we do not have wisdom to see it in God, then we will find whatever substitute that feeds our false egos in the world. This will eventually lead to the death of our souls and to physical death as well.

A FEW QUOTES TO MEDITATE ON

Lao Tzu encourages us, "The journey of a thousand miles begins with one step." George Bernard Shaw said, "We are made wise not by the recollection of our past but by the responsibility of our future." Lucius Annaeus Seneca said, "No man was ever wise by chance." Finally, Aristotle said, "We are what we repeatedly do. Excellence, then, is not an act, but a habit."

My friends, as believers of Christ, anchor all your confidence in the word of God, the only source of true wisdom. You will never be misled but instead will be fulfilled and enriched with the fruit of the spirit.

List Ways That Your Life Will Be Better as a Result of Empowering Your Mind with Wisdom from the Word of God

_____

_____

_____

_____

_____

_____

_____

_____

_____

_____

_____

HEALTH TIP #25: **Cleanse Your Kidneys**

The kidneys are one of the most important organs in our body, and it's vital to take care of them. They filter toxins in the system that can be dangerous to our health. And I know you all have heard the saying, "We are what we eat," so please be good to yourself. Cranberry juice helps to detoxify the kidneys as they aid in the removing of excess calcium oxalate. Beet juice and lemon juice also help remove toxins that may build up into kidney stones.

Avocado leaves are known to detoxify and help cleanse the kidneys to help them function in their best fashion, and they can be taken in a drink mixture. There are also kidney cleanses that are sold at the health food stores. Talk to a health professional about this.

DAY 26

IT IS GOD'S INTENTION THAT WE REPRESENT HIM

Donnie McClurkin wrote a song that makes my soul weep! He starts out by asking God these questions: "Lord where will I go without your hand holding me? And how could I live without you I can't see, Lord. What will I do in life? Where will I go? How would I handle things?" These are very important questions to ask ourselves. I personally think that I would certainly be lost! I truly Love the Lord. God wants us to hunger after Him. He wants us to live our lives to glorify Him and honor Him.

Jesus was once asked which commandment of the Law was the greatest. Matthew 22:37 (NIV) says, "Jesus replied: "'Love the Lord your God with all your heart and with all your soul and with all your mind.' This is the first and greatest commandment. And the second is like it: 'Love your neighbor as yourself.' All the Law and the Prophets hang on these two commandments."

As Christians, we represent Christ, and we are called to be His ambassadors. This mandates that we are to take on Christ-like characteristics. As believers, our lives must be noticeably different from the nonbelievers. We have a responsibility to demonstrate to the world who Jesus is through our words and actions. He has given us an incredible gift, the gift of his death and resurrection. If someone gave their life for you, how would you treat them in return? God has an undying, powerful love for us, what we call agape love, and in return, He has called us to be like Him—to live our lives in such a way that we can show his love to those we have encountered. My brother started a ministry years ago where he would feed the homeless. Every Friday we would get together and prepare food for the people in the shelters. We would also walk the streets and hand out blankets, food, and something to drink. We prayed and ministered the gospel to them. Some would curse at us, but we never let anything discourage us. We had one reason in mind, and it was for the love of Jesus Christ.

In the letter to the Corinthians, the apostle Paul discusses the ministry of reconciliation, and he uses the term *ambassadors* for Christ. Let's take a look at the word and its meaning. An ambassador is a respected official acting as a representative of a nation. Sent to a foreign land, the ambassador's role is to reflect the official position of the sovereign body that gave them the authority. Paul likens his own calling to that of an ambassador for Christ, and he urges all Christians to do the same.

God wants us to have a personal, one-on-one relationship with Him. He wants to speak to us, not only so that we may draw nearer to Him, but that we may also be living proof of His goodness and mercy.

John 10:27–28 (NIV) says, "My sheep listen to My voice; I know them, and they follow Me. I give them eternal life, and they shall never perish; no one will snatch them out of My hand."

In Jeremiah 7:23–24 (NIV), the Bible says, "But I gave them this command: Obey me, and I will be your God and you will be My people. Walk in obedience to all I command you, that it may go well with you. But they did not listen or pay attention; instead, they followed the stubborn inclinations of their evil hearts. They went backward and not forward."

Knowing God is a lifetime journey of prayer, Bible study, and obedience. When we know God, we know what delights Him. God's intention is for man to represent Him with His authority. In Romans 5:17 (NIV), Paul writes, "For if, by the trespass of the one man, death reigned through that one man, how much more will those who receive God's abundant provision of grace and of the gift of righteousness reign in life through the one man, Jesus Christ!"

Christ has also given us authority to rule over Satan. In Luke 10:19 (NIV), the Bible explains, "I have given you authority to trample on snakes and scorpions and to overcome all the power of the enemy; nothing will harm you." People of God, our weapon is knowing the word of God. And it is my sincere desire for you to really study the Word. Memorize scriptures so that when the enemy comes at you, you will be able to stand on God's promises to us. Knowledge is power.

Shannon L. Alder's quote on representing God is very powerful and relevant in our lives. "The most compassionate and peaceful thing you can do for yourself and others is to let go of the past, let go of the anger, let go of trying to hurt people that wronged you. There are thousands of people dying from cancer that wish they had someone to care about them and be with them during their final days. There are children being sold into sex trafficking and are hoping someone would rescue them. There are homeless people that wish they had something warm to wear or eat. There is an entire species being wiped out because not enough people care about our oceans. Today, remember that there is someone praying for the very things you take for granted. Spend your effort where God needs you to be - on the front lines of the war on earth, not on the battlefields of the past." Powerful words of advice!

This is a story to remind you all to honor your time and others, because you represent God through your actions. We must stop the arguing, fussing, and fighting, because we never know when the end is near.

Recently I received a call from a young lady in my ministry, she called and asked me to pray for her friends she had gone to visit. She was in tears. As she continued talking, she said that they had been married for more than fifteen years and lately all they seemed to want to do was argue with each other. There had been talks of divorce. So the couple decided to separate themselves for three weeks. She was going to visit their daughter who lives in another state while her husband relaxed at home and did what he loves to do. All this was being told to me by the young lady I will call Angel.

I, on the other hand, was talking to both the husband and wife on speaker. I expressed to them how time is short, and they should quit arguing and begin praying. I even suggested counseling for the couple. They agreed for counseling, made up, and were on good terms again. I prayed with them and told Angel to be sure to talk to them about Jesus.

Approximately two hours later Angel called back and told

me that the gentleman had passed. He simply had a massive heart attack and died instantly. His wife was devastated! Now he was gone for a permanent separation! Life is short; please use your time wisely. There is no need to spend our lives fighting and arguing with anyone. If you are, choose to stop this day!

By letting go of all the negative emotions that we've been carrying, and focusing on God and His instructions, we are able to represent Christ in the best way. Think of all the things we are called to do: to serve God's people, to preach and teach the gospel, to reach out to each other in need with no expectation in return, to be givers. Focus on God's direction for your life.

In John 21:17 (NIV), we see, "The third time he said to him, 'Simon son of John, do you love me?'" Peter was hurt because Jesus asked him the third time, "Do you love me?" He said, "Lord, you know all things; you know that I love you." Jesus said, "Feed my sheep." Oh, glory to God!

As Christ's ambassadors, we are to value people as Jesus did! We are called to be members of a royal priesthood. In the Bible, 1 Peter 2:9 (NIV) says, "But you are a chosen people, a royal priesthood, a holy nation, God's special possession, that you may declare the praises of him who called you out of darkness into his wonderful light."

We are selected from among humanity and are developed to understand, sympathize and deal gently with others since we have similar weaknesses and failings.

In Hebrews 5:1–3 (NIV), the Bible further explains, "Every high priest is selected from among the people and is appointed to represent the people in matters related to God, to offer gifts and sacrifices for sins. He is able to deal gently with those who are ignorant and are going astray, since he himself is subject to weakness. This is why he has to offer sacrifices for his own sins, as well as for the sins of the people."

Jesus reminds us in his Word, Matthew 5:14–16 (NIV), "You are the light of the world. A town built on a hill cannot be hidden. Neither do people light a lamp and put it under a bowl. Instead, they put it on its stand, and it gives light to everyone in the house. In the same way, let your light shine before others, that they may see your good deeds and glorify your Father in heaven." Oh, how I love the word of God! It is simply love songs for my soul.

We are to be a light for people in a dark world, to be a pathway for others to want to create their own relationship with Christ Jesus. When people see your light and the fruit you bear, they too will want to honor and glorify God.

In 2 Timothy 4:1–5 (NIV), the Bible explains, "In the presence of God and of Christ Jesus, who will judge the living and the dead, and in view of his appearing and his kingdom, I give you this charge: Preach the word; be prepared in season and out of season; correct, rebuke and encourage - with great patience and careful instruction. For the time will come when people will not put up with sound doctrine. Instead, to suit their own desires, they will gather around them a great number of teachers to say what their itching ears want to hear. They will turn their ears away from the truth and turn aside to myths. But you, keep your head in all situations, endure hardship, do the work of an evangelist, discharge all the duties of your ministry."

Hebrews 12:15 (NIV) says, "See to it that no one falls short of the grace of God and that no bitter root grows up to cause trouble and defile many."

Luke 6:46–49 (NIV) explains that Jesus said, "Why do you call me, 'Lord, Lord,' and do not do what I say? As for everyone who comes to Me and hears My words and puts them into practice, I will show you what they are like. They are like a man building a house, who dug down deep and laid the foundation on rock. When a flood came, the torrent struck that house but could not shake it, because it was well built. But the one who hears My words and does not put them into practice is like a man who built a house on the ground without a foundation. The moment the torrent struck that house, it collapsed and its destruction was complete."

Jesus places emphasis on action, on "doing," by saying it was vain to call Him Lord while not following His instruction.

The reason Jesus came in the flesh was for the benefit of others, so that human beings could have their sins forgiven through the sacrifice of his perfect life. Jesus drew attention to that fact when the disciples began to worry about who was going to get the highest position of honor in the kingdom. Mark 10:42–45 (NIV) reveals, "Jesus called them together and said, 'You know that those who are regarded as rulers of the Gentiles lord it over them, and their high officials exercise authority over them. Not so with you. Instead, whoever wants to become great among you, must be your servant, and whoever wants to be first must be slave of all. For even the Son of Man did not come to be served, but to serve, and to give his life as a ransom for many.'"

Glory to God! Friends, it is imperative that we represent him in truth and holiness! The world needs truth!

How Are You Serving as God's Ambassador Here on Earth?

_____

_____

_____

_____

_____

_____

_____

_____

_____

_____

_____

HEALTH TIP #26: **Beautiful Skin**

One of my favorite things to do is to assemble my very own facial mask consisting of bentonite clay, apple cider vinegar, and a few drops of rose absolute oil. I mix them together to form a paste and apply it to my face. This is by far one of my favorite beauty secrets. Applying this mixture will remove dark spots from the face, tighten the skin, close large pores, and simply make your skin more beautiful and impart a youthful glow.

Bentonite clay is formed from different minerals in volcanic ash and is a natural healing agent. It's very powerful and, when added to water, creates a negative electric charge that allows it to become a powerful tool for absorbing toxins. I have also recommended this as a colon cleanse. High-quality bentonite clay is safe to consume and is great for the colon. It is also known to remove heavy metals in the body.

DAY 27

YOUR TRUE CHARACTER IS WHAT YOU ARE WHEN NOBODY'S WATCHING

Years ago I needed to take a trip to New York City, so to lower the cost of my trip, I agreed to carpool with a friend's distant cousin. Halfway to our destination, we decided to stop for food and a bathroom break. Because the woman did not want to dine in, we decided to grab our food and head back on the road. To my amazement, when we finished our food she grabbed our trash and threw it out of the window. I was very upset and told her that it was unethical and wrong to act in such manner. She then proceeded to challenge my opinion saying, "It doesn't matter! No one cares!" I beg to differ!

Jesus said that we will be judged on how we behave in small and apparently insignificant things. "Whoever can be trusted with very little can also be trusted with much, and whoever is dishonest with very little will also be dishonest with much" (Luke 16:10 NIV).

Many writers have said that character is what you are when no one is looking. As I searched further, I found a similar quotation with additional attributes: "You can easily judge the character of a man by how he treats those who can do nothing for him." My friends we must consider everyone's work. Even the janitor that cleans the streets. Honor and respect for every persons and things are very important. One should never think of himself so highly that he finds the need to dishonor his fellow man.

So, you ask, "What is character?" A person's character is who they are, the qualities they possess. As humans we are called to humble ourselves. For me I ask this question to myself quite often. Are you honest and fair in your dealings with humanity?

Character is the aggregate of a person's ethical and moral qualities, and it is demonstrated through the choices and actions we make. A person of good character is someone who acts morally and ethically upright, and that is mindful of others. I'm not saying that to have "good" character a person must never make mistakes, because we have all fallen short in one way or another. Rather, a person of good character is someone who is constantly striving to be better in all aspects of their lives. When this person recognizes they have done something wrong, they do what is necessary to get back on track.

It is said that there are three types of people in the world: givers (those who help others not expecting anything in return), takers (those who help themselves, selfish), and matchers (those who seek equal benefit for themselves and others).

The givers were found to be the most successful of the three because they bring out the best in others. These individuals give without a motive. In my opinion they mimic the characteristics of God. Givers help secure their own success. They often look at the people around them as diamonds in the rough and are encouragers. These individuals possess the greatest character and qualities of unwavering commitment and resilience.

Nelson Mandela, a man I have great respect for, said, "The greatest glory in living lies not in never falling, but rising every time we fall."

Admit it when you have made a mistake and be open for godly correction. Ask for forgiveness and move on. We can only grow and become better in our shortcomings and pains.

Abraham Lincoln once said, "Character is like a tree and reputation like its shadow. The shadow is what we think of it; The tree is the real thing." Your character is the real you in the sense that you cannot separate what you do from who you are.

The list of high-value character traits is extensive and includes things such as integrity, courage, and fortitude. In addition to the many noble traits the Bible says, "But the fruit of the Spirit is love, joy, peace, forbearance, kindness, goodness, faithfulness, gentleness and self-control. Against such things there is no law" (Galatians 5:22–23 NIV).

God has been directing man to the path of morality through his word. The definitive direction is written in the Ten Commandments. Here it is:

> You shall not misuse the name of the Lord your God, for the Lord will not hold anyone guiltless who misuses his name. Remember the Sabbath day by keeping it holy. Six days you shall labor and do all your work, but the seventh day is a Sabbath to the Lord your God. On it you shall not do any work, neither you, nor your son or daughter, nor your male or female servant, nor your animals, nor any foreigner residing in your towns. For in six days, the

Lord made the heavens and the earth, the sea, and all that is in them, but he rested on the seventh day. Therefore, the Lord blessed the Sabbath day and made it holy. Honor your father and your mother, so that you may live long in the land the Lord your God is giving you. You shall not murder. You shall not commit adultery. You shall not steal. You shall not give false testimony against your neighbor. You shall not covet your neighbor's house. You shall not covet your neighbor's wife, or his male or female servant, his ox or donkey, or anything that belongs to your neighbor. (Exodus 20:7-17 NIV)

Clearly, God's word is filled with the guidelines concerning how a person with godly character is to think and act. He further instructs us, "Finally, brothers and sisters, whatever is true, whatever is noble, whatever is right, whatever is pure, whatever is lovely, whatever is admirable—if anything is excellent or praiseworthy—think about such things. Whatever you have learned or received or heard from Me, or seen in Me—put it into practice. And the God of peace will be with you." (Philippians 4:8-9 NIV). Thinking on all things good and holy is also a good way to show gratitude and thus bring more blessing and goodness into your life.

One of the great lessons Jesus taught his followers is that a man's or woman's character is always a matter of what is in his or her heart. That is why God tells us that we are to guard our hearts, to protect them with the greatest of care.

In Proverbs 4:23 (NIV), the Bible says, "Above all else, guard your heart, for everything you do flows from it." In Jeremiah 17:9–10 (NIV), the Bible also explains, "The heart is deceitful above all things and beyond cure. Who can understand it? I the Lord search the heart and examine the mind, to reward each person according to their conduct, according to what their deeds deserve."

In 1 Corinthians 4:5 (NIV), Paul writes, "Therefore judge nothing before the appointed time; wait until the Lord comes. He will bring to light what is hidden in darkness and will expose the motives of the heart. At that time, each will receive their praise from God." In Proverbs 21:2 (NIV), the Bible says, "A person may think their own ways are right, but the Lord weighs the heart."

Every action you take will be judged by God. Beloved, remember each of us will stand before the judgment seat of Christ, where our hearts, our character, our thoughts, and deeds will be exposed. In 2 Corinthians 5:10 (NIV), we learn, "For we must all appear before the judgment seat of Christ, so that each of us may receive what is due us for the things done while in the body, whether good or bad."

My brothers and sisters, today we can choose to change the negative habits that are disabling our growth. The choice is ours and ours alone—we can go before our Lord and Savior and ask Him to change us to be more like Him. We must ask Him to give us a heart to feel the pain of others and to be able to sympathize with the ones who hurt.

Pray that the Lord transforms your character so that it mimics the character of Christ. Put it into practice and watch God do great and mighty things through you.

In Ezekiel 18:30–32 (NIV), the Bible says, "'Therefore, you Israelites, I will judge each of you according to your own ways,' declares the Sovereign Lord. 'Repent! Turn away from all your offenses; then sin will not be your downfall. Rid yourselves of all the offenses you have committed, and get a new heart and a new spirit. Why will you die, people of Israel? For I take no pleasure in the death of anyone,' declares the Sovereign Lord. Repent and live!"

Here our Sovereign Lord warns us to repent and turn from our foolish ways. Abraham Lincoln once said, "Nearly all men can stand adversity, but if you want to test a man's character, give him power."

Another illustrative quote is by Zig Ziglar, a motivational speaker: "The foundation stones for a balanced success are honesty, character, integrity, faith, love and loyalty."

Lolly Daskal, a leadership executive coach, said, "The moments that define who we truly are created when nobody's watching. When our heart pushes us to do something simply because it calls to be done. That is someone who leads when nobody's watching. When your soul aches to be seen and your voice to be heard, you have become passionate—even though no one is watching. When you reach for a level of excellence that makes your heart smile, you have become disciplined—even though no one is watching … Every one of us can look toward the stars. Every one of us can shine. Who are you when nobody's watching? Those are the moments when you're defining yourself. Those moments when the only reward is choosing to do something for no other reason than to prove to yourself that you could do it—to prove that you can be extraordinary."

Divine character is when you know from within that you have done the work, and finally you possess the qualities of our Lord and Savior, Jesus Christ.

Ask Yourself How Much You Are Willing to Sacrifice for Someone Who Can Do Nothing for You in Return.

Make a List of Your Character Defects and How
You Can Turn Them into Something Positive.

_____

_____

_____

_____

_____

_____

_____

_____

_____

_____

_____

_____

HEALTH TIP #27: **How to Make Tooth Pain Disappear in a Flash**

You should make an appointment with a dentist as soon as possible if you're in constant pain. However, if you find yourself in a situation and need temporary tooth pain relief, application of clove oil may help.

Pure clove oil is very powerful and, when used at full strength, has the ability to burn your skin or cause nausea. Dilute it with olive oil (one part clove oil, two parts olive oil). Be sure to use a high quality pure essential oil.

After mixing, do a skin test to determine if you are allergic to cloves. Apply a small amount to your skin, with the best testing area being the inside of your forearm, and wait. If any rash appears, it would be advisable to seek an alternative treatment.

Using a Q-tip, dip it into the oil mixture and put it directly onto the tooth that is in pain. You can repeat this as often as needed until you get to your dentist.

DAY 28

LET YOUR WORD BE YOUR BOND

When I was growing up, I often heard my father say, "Let your word be your bond," and, "If you do not have your word, you have nothing!" Although at the time the meaning and purpose of those words was lost on my young mind, I have thankfully grown to recognize their wisdom and have chosen to honor them through my actions. To me, these words have become a universal sign of honor that when you promise to do something, you must follow through!

As a child, when I asked my father to do something or buy me perhaps a toy or an outfit, he looked me in the eyes and told me that he couldn't promise to do anything if he was not able. He further explained that promises or offers to help should not be taken lightly, and that a person with integrity doesn't rashly speak vain words that sound good at the time just to get someone off their back.

If you do not intend to follow through with a promise, do not give your word. On the other hand, if you make a promise or say you will do something, whether it be of great or small importance, it should be done.

The responsible person will carefully think about his or her ability and dedication to fulfil his or her promise before the responsible person gives his or her word. From the conversations

I have with people during the course of my ministry, I can honestly tell you that you can almost always tell a person's character by the words that they speak. Some people talk a good talk, telling you everything it is that they think you want to hear, but then, they end up not being true to their word. As for me, I have learned to keep these types of people at an arm's length.

The words we speak are powerful, and as a chosen people we must know this! Jesus Christ emphasized the power of the word! In Matthew 12:37 (NIV), He said, "For by your words you will be acquitted, and by your words you will be condemned." In Proverbs 18:21 (NIV), the Bible explains, "Death and life are in the power of the tongue: and they that love it shall eat the fruit thereof." Therefore, the content of what we say must be trusted.

According to Van Waller, an empowerment speaker, "Every time you give someone your word, your reputation and standard of personal integrity is on the line. You will never be truly successful without a high regard for your own personal integrity."

Werner Erhard said, "Honoring your word is also the route to creating whole and complete social and working relationships. In addition, it provides an actionable pathway to earning the trust of others."

James 1:27 (NIV) says, "Religion that God our Father accepts as pure and faultless is this: to look after orphans and widows in their distress and to keep oneself from being polluted by the world." In Malachi 2:2 (NIV), the Bible also says, "'If you do not listen, and if you do not resolve to honor my name,' says the Lord Almighty, 'I will send a curse on you, and I will curse your blessings. Yes, I have already cursed them, because you have not resolved to honor me.'"

In 2 Peter 1:17 (NIV), we learn, "He received honor and glory from God the Father when the voice came to him from the Majestic Glory, saying, 'This is my Son, whom I love; with him I am well pleased.'"

This is what the Lord said: "Be devoted to one another in love. Honor one another above yourselves." And in Philippians 2:3 (NIV), we are instructed, "Do nothing out of selfish ambition or vain conceit. Rather, in humility value others above yourselves."

Can Your Words Be Trusted? Examine Your Track Record. What Does It Look Like?

_____

_____

_____

_____

_____

_____

_____

_____

_____

_____

_____

_____

HEALTH TIP #28: **Experiencing Swelling in the Feet, Hands, Ankles, and Legs?**

According to *Health and Healthy Living*, water retention, also known as edema, is the accumulation of fluids in the tissues and cavities as well as the circulatory system.

Here are a few causes:

1. Inactivity
2. Taking medication for a long period of time
3. Excessive intake of salt
4. Magnesium deficiency
5. Potassium deficiency
6. Excessive consumption of processed foods

Beneficial Herbs for Reducing Edema (should be taken as directed):

1. Dandelion
2. Horsetail
3. Parsley
4. Garlic
5. Also check your water consumption. Are you drinking enough water?

DAY 29

WHEN THE ENEMY COMES IN LIKE A FLOOD, GOD WILL RAISE UP A STANDARD

The God we serve is a mighty warrior! In Revelation 19:11–16 (NIV), scripture tells, "I saw heaven standing open and there before me was a white horse, whose rider is called Faithful and True. With justice, he judges and wages war. His eyes are like blazing fire, and on his head are many crowns. He has a name written on him that no one knows but he himself. He is dressed in a robe dipped in blood, and his name is the Word of God. The armies of heaven were following him, riding on white horses and dressed in fine linen, white and clean. Coming out of his mouth is a sharp sword with which to strike down the nations. 'He will rule them with an iron scepter.' He treads the winepress of the fury of the wrath of God Almighty. On his robe and on his thigh he has this name written: King of Kings and Lord of Lords." Oh Glory!

Today I want to speak a word of peace over your life. My beloved, when the enemy comes in like a flood, God will raise up a standard. He said in His word that He will make your enemy your footstool. When the enemy tries to attack you, God will encamp His angels to fight for you.

Trust Him with all of your heart. If you are going through a dire situation, trust God in it. For over thirty-five years, I have been a believer and I have never seen the righteous forsaken. There have been many times I have gone through trials, endured the worst of situations, and encountered tests and battles, but I have remained steadfast, for scripture says, "Whoever dwells in the shelter of the Most High will rest in the shadow of the Almighty. God warned us saying, "From the west, people will fear the name of the Lord, and from the rising of the sun, they will revere His glory. For He will come like a pent-up flood that the breath of the Lord drives along."

Please understand that the attacks we experience are spiritual. The word of God says, "For our struggle is not against flesh and blood, but against the rulers, against the authorities, against the powers of this dark world and against the spiritual forces of evil in the heavenly realms."

Our true enemy is not people, finance, or other physical obstacles of any kind. The root cause of our troubles is a spiritual agenda whose goal is to stop us from doing the things that are infringing on the kingdom of darkness. Whether the spiritual attack is on ourselves, our children, family, or friends, we must understand the word of God for ourselves.

If we are going to fight a spiritual battle, we have to use the weapons that work in that realm. These weapons are prayers, fasting, and the Word of God. When it seems we are being attacked from all directions, we must intensify the fight through an increase in praying and fasting. The Word of God will reinforce your faith and give you strength. Remember: you cannot do this alone, and without Jesus, we are nothing—we have no strength! Let the Lord win this battle for you.

I recently read an article in *Christian Mingle*, and the author said, "One of the greatest temptations and mistakes that I have faced has been when I have given up when things were getting hot. I have learned that many times the battle rages the fiercest when the victory is almost won. You need to understand that the enemy of our souls has an intense hatred for anyone that will follow Jesus wholeheartedly." He is threatened by the fact that we are able to win souls for Jesus. Remember his intentions are to steal kill and destroy.

"He will not just lay over like a beaten coward and expose himself at the first sign of battle. He goes around as a roaring lion, looking for whomever he can devour." Let's strike him down with the word of God!

Deuteronomy 20:1 (NIV) says, "When you go to war against your enemies and see horses and chariots and an army greater than yours, do not be afraid of them, because the Lord your God, who brought you up out of Egypt, will be with you."

Remember the Lord said, "I will bless those who bless you, and whoever curses you I will curse; and all peoples on earth will be blessed through you." God will invoke the supernatural powers of heaven for you to bring victory. So be not discourage your heavenly Father sees everything. Hold on to him, grab onto his garment and pray.

A perfect example would be on the day that David went to meet his three older brothers who were fighting in the army of Saul against the Philistine warrior. David knew that Goliath had no covenant protection from God, so, filled with a holy indignation, he decided to face the giant himself. He refused the king's armor, for it did not fit him. And I believe this would have slowed him down. So he met Goliath on the field of battle with the holy armor of God.

David spoke with confidence in his God: "This day the Lord will deliver you into my hands, and I'll strike you down and cut off your head. This very day I will give the carcasses of the Philistine army to the birds and the wild animals, and the whole world will know that there is a God in Israel" (1 Samuel 17:46 NIV). Amen. I don't know about you but this right here deserves a shout of praise.

Sing praises to His name, oh, people of Zion, for our Redeemer lives. And in Him your battle is already won.

How Do You Plan on Slaying Your Goliath?

_____

_____

_____

_____

_____

_____

_____

_____

_____

_____

_____

Are You Fighting with Strength and Might in Jesus's Name?

_____

_____

_____

_____

_____

_____

_____

_____

_____

_____

_____

_____

HEALTH TIP #29: **Want to Restore the Natural Balance of the pH Levels in Your Body?**

The combination of pure, natural honey and apple cider vinegar will restore the natural balance of pH levels in your body. And as I mentioned earlier, liquid chlorophyll is my favorite. These are just a few. There are many more that will aid in this process. So having a balance PH system is a must! As a result, you will experience these wonderful health benefits: possible relief of joint pain, digestive issues, and muscle pain; promotion of weight loss; and boosting of energy. It will help with bad breath and help digestion and constipation. So it's important to know your pH level in your body.

Apple cider vinegar is high in potassium, niacin, folic acid, magnesium, calcium, iron, citric acid, and vitamins C, B6, B1, and B2. Pure organic honey is rich in iron, vitamin C, zinc, calcium, copper, potassium, magnesium, vitamin B6, thiamine, riboflavin, pantothenic acid, and nicotinic acid. When mixed together, they create a powerful cleanse that nourishes and replenishes the body.

To make the mixture of apple cider vinegar and honey, add one teaspoon of pure natural honey and a teaspoon of apple cider vinegar to a cup of water. Mix well and drink on an empty stomach before breakfast. (Visit healthadvisorgroup.com for more information.)

DAY 30

NOT EVERYONE THAT STARTS WITH YOU WILL FINISH WITH YOU

Though it may be painful, sometimes you have to evaluate the people who are around you, especially those who are in your close circle. A large measure of your success comes down to the people you spend time with. Keep in mind: the people you are around determine how you think, how you act, and ultimately, how successful you will be. Do not allow your spirit to be polluted with stinking thinking. Run from people who are always negative!

In my life experiences, I have had to make some tough decisions in removing myself from people I have known for decades—even to the point of including a few family members.

I was in an intensely abusive relationship for many years, and the stress and anguish of the abuse seriously impacted my physical, emotional, and mental health. When I entered into the relationship, I had every intention of fulfilling my vows. However, the actions of my significant other toward me and his behavior in the larger world put me into a serious dilemma. I tried my very best to try to repair the wounds and maintain my sanity, all the while raising my children and trying to keep them from also becoming victims. The massive amount of strain and stress, delivered over an extended period of time, caused my being to deteriorate and made me doubt whether I wanted to continue to live.

It was at this point that I did something that was the farthest from my intentions. I left the relationship to rid myself of an abusive man to save my own life and the lives of our children.

I remember that though the separation was painful, I had to distance myself because, if not, the relationship would have taken me down a path from which there was guarantee no return. To this day, I still get emotional when I think about my decision. I would have died had I not removed myself from this dreadful place. I learned a most valuable lesson from that—at times, you need to break off relationships with others that are not helping you along your journey to your destiny. Though it may not be easy, it is necessary.

In subsequent years, I've come to firmly realize that not everyone with whom you create a relationship has your best interests at hand. Be they personal, business, or romantic relationships, I have had to face the painful fact that not everyone that starts with you will finish with you. I have had to ask myself if these would be the people that would stay with me through life's journey. Frankly, some answers horrified me. Do not live with people who do not believe in you.

One of the biggest factors in getting refueled and staying refueled is deciding who you allow to influence you. Consider the voices around you! The book of Proverbs makes it clear that not only will we encounter people who are wise and supportive to our lives' missions, but also we will encounter people who are unwise and detrimental or destructive to our lives' missions.

Our destination in life in large part is determined by the choices we make on those that are closest to us. One of the biggest factors that drains people's energy is not wisely dealing with difficult, distracting people. It is absolutely essential to surround ourselves with ingenious, reinforcing, and reinvigorating people.

Proverbs 13:20 (NIV) says, "Walk with the wise and become wise, for a companion of fools suffers harm." If you allow wise people into your inner circle, you in turn will become wiser.

I have had to resort to terminating relationships with many with whom I'd become close. Though it was difficult, I took comfort in knowing that breaking things off would be best for me in the long run. We have to be aware and realize that for periods in this life, we are called to walk our journey alone.

Have you ever heard the saying, "Show me your friends, I will tell you who you are"? Indeed, it is so! On the other hand, expect harm to come into your life if you allow people who consistently make foolish decisions.

If you want to know what is in store for you look around at the people who you are closest to, the people whose opinion you value the most. What your associates think, do, and say will be what you mimic. Proverbs 14:7 (NIV) says, "Stay away from a fool, for you will not find knowledge on their lips."1 Corinthians 15:33 (NIV) says, "Do not be misled: 'Bad company corrupts good character.'"

Truth is, you are only going to be as great as the ones you

surround yourself with; be brave and let go of the people who are weighing you down. I recall trying to help someone. I knew this person did not have good credit, so I helped this person by purchasing something the person needed. Even though they made payments to pay off what was bought, it was not always on time. You see, if they did not care about their own credit, why would I expect them to care about mine? Be careful who you trust!

One of my favorite quotes is, "Of all the relationships we have, it is our friends who most directly reveal the kind of person we are. If you want to understand someone, you only have to look at their circle of friends, which will tell you what their values and priorities are." (Yu Dan.Confucius from the Heart: Ancient Wisdom for Today's World). Don't be suckered into a relationship that is a lie. Be wise, watch, and listen carefully. Allow God to lead and guide you. God wants the best for you and in return He wants you to choose people that will honor the greatness in you as your father in heaven does. Respect yourself. Do not dumb yourself down for anyone. You are a child of the King and must be treated as such!

Finally, it is absolutely necessary to surround ourselves with the dreamers and doers, the believers and thinkers. More importantly, surround yourself with those who see greatness within you and believe in you even when you cannot see it in yourself. All through the comings and goings and changes of relationships, I have steadfastly continued to hold on to Jesus, who I knew would never fail me. Remember: in spite of everything going on about us, God is always with us.

In Proverbs 15:1–5 (NIV), the Bible instructs us, "A gentle

answer turns away wrath, but a harsh word stirs up anger. The tongue of the wise adorns knowledge, but the mouth of the fool gushes folly. The eyes of the Lord are everywhere, keeping watch on the wicked and the good. The soothing tongue is a tree of life, but a perverse tongue crushes the spirit. A fool spurns a parent's discipline, but whoever heeds correction shows prudence."

Ask the Lord to remove that which does not belong and to sever all illegal relationships that are there to cause you harm. Pray that your heavenly Father will send you people that will propel you into your destiny in Jesus's name!

Are Those You Choose to Spend Time with Hindering or Helping Your Life's Mission?

_____

_____

_____

_____

_____

_____

_____

_____

_____

_____

_____

What Changes Do You Need to Make in Your Associates in Order to Ensure a Better Future?

_____

_____

_____

_____

_____

_____

_____

_____

_____

_____

_____

HEALTH TIP #30: **Oral Health**

Maintaining your oral health is important because it has a tremendous effect on your overall well-being. Mouth infections can lead to major internal organ problems like heart attacks, strokes, pancreatic cancer, kidney disease, and digestion problems, just to name a few. The best way to help avoid these health problems is to upkeep and take care of your oral health, a good first step would be oil pulling.

Oil pulling is a treatment in which you swish coconut oil in your mouth for several minutes. It's been shown to improve oral health by removing toxins and infections, dangerous bacteria, strengthening the gums, and also helps whiten teeth. Some studies have shown it to also treat other ailments from liver problems, hormonal imbalances, skin health, and more.

Be sure to use good quality coconut oil, which is known as an antifungal.

In the morning, before brushing your teeth, swish a few teaspoons of organic coconut oil in your mouth for a couple minutes. Once done, spit it out but don't swallow it, as it is filled with the bacteria and toxins that once thrived in your mouth. Rinse your mouth with warm water and brush your teeth as usual to remove any leftover bacteria. I myself have tried oil pulling and it has become a daily routine. I recommend trying it for yourself you have nothing to lose but gain. In my private practice, many of my clients have tried it and absolutely love the result.

DAY 31

LORD, I AM WEAK, BUT YOU ARE STRONG

I became pregnant out of wedlock and felt alone. I was only eighteen; my mother urged me to abort my baby; whereas, I wanted to keep him. I remember the feeling of being helpless against my mother's command at the thought of aborting my baby! She thought I would bring her shame by being pregnant, so as to avoid it, she took me to the abortion clinic to terminate the gift God had given me.

I was despondent and thought I had no other choice but to go along with my mother's desire. I was under her leadership and had to do as I was told. As I sat in the doctor's office waiting for my procedure, I prayed, "God, I am weak but you are strong! Please help me. I want to keep my baby!"

God heard me. The doctor came into the room, and after one look at me, he recoiled, fear written all over his face. He told me to put my clothes back on and stated that he refused to perform the procedure on me. Keep in mind, I said not a word to him. The doctor even offered me a refund of the money my mother had paid!

Despite my mother being upset, God ultimately had a plan for me and my unborn child. Today, he is twenty-nine years old and is one of the loves of my life, my gift from God, my beloved son. I am grateful and thankful for him. God saw fit to bless me with two additional amazing angels. I thank him for favoring me with them! I am humbled and grateful. But looking back, I often wonder why the doctor stepped away from me in fear. If I had a chance to talk to him, I would ask him what made him refuse to perform the procedure on me? To this day I am still amazed!

This reminds me of the story of Daniel in the lion's den! The story relates how Daniel not only gained favor with King Darius but also was raised to high office because he was a hard worker and extremely honest. He was also very obedient to his God, Yahweh, Jehovah, the God of Israel. Because he achieved the position of administrator among the political ranks, the local officials were angry and jealous. We will always have haters so his haters conspired a plot to remove him from his position of prominent authority. The officials convinced the king to issue a decree that stated if anyone was caught praying to another god or man besides the king, during a specific thirty-day period, they would be thrown into the lion's den. Daniel would not stop praying to his God, so he was thrown into the lion's den.

King Darius believed that the lions would devour Daniel, and for this reason, he would neither eat nor sleep. The next morning, the king learned that Daniel was still alive and hurried to the den to see if it was true.

When the king saw that Daniel was, in fact, alive and unscathed, he asked Daniel if his God had protected him. Daniel answered and said, "My God sent his angel, and he shut the mouths of the lions. They have not hurt me, because I was found innocent in his sight. Nor have I ever done any wrong before you, Your Majesty" (Daniel 6:22 NIV).

People of God, let us strengthen our faith and fear not. Daniel was eventually vindicated, and the ones who had plotted against him were thrown, along with their wives and children, into the lion's den as punishment. It was said that before they reached the floor of the den, the lions overpowered them and crushed all their bones.

"Then King Darius wrote to all the nations and peoples of every language in all the earth: 'May you prosper greatly! I issue a decree that in every part of my kingdom people must fear and show reverence to the God of Daniel. For he is the living God and he endures forever; His kingdom will not be destroyed, His dominion will never end. He rescues and He saves; He performs signs and wonders in the heavens and on the earth. He has rescued Daniel from the power of the lions.' So Daniel prospered during the reign of Darius and the reign of Cyrus the Persian." (Daniel 6:25-28 NIV). People of God our Redeemer lives!

My friends, just reading the story of Daniel makes me surrender to Jesus! God is indeed a mighty warrior and a defender. Pray earnestly and tell Him you are weak but He is strong. Call Him, for He will answer.

In Isaiah 43:1–3 (NIV), the Bible explains, "But now, this is what the Lord says— he who created you, Jacob, he who formed you, Israel: "Do not fear, for I have redeemed you; I have summoned you by name; you are mine. When you pass through the waters, I will be with you; and when you pass through the rivers, they will not sweep over you. When you walk through the fire, you will not be burned; the flames will not set you ablaze. For I am the Lord your God, the Holy One of Israel, your Savior."

Study the Story of Daniel in Its Entirety and Relate How the Story Pertains to You

_____

_____

_____

_____

_____

_____

_____

_____

_____

_____

_____

_____

HEALTH TIP #31: **Do You Have an Abscess?**

An abscess is a localized collection of pus in a part of the body formed by tissue disintegration and surrounded by an inflamed area. These are suggestions of things to use:

1. Black Ointment (healing drawing salve). You can use this product externally by applying directly on affected area until the abscess opens. I have tried this on pets and got great results too.
2. Golden Salve
3. Silver Shield (anti-bacterial)
4. Essential oils that are recommended:
    a. Tea tree, frankincense, or helichrysum will bring the abscess to a head.
    b. Thyme, myrrh, or frankincense will dry and close the open abscess.

DAY 32

BOUNDARIES ARE IMPORTANT FOR GROWTH FOR YOUR WELL BEING

Establishing boundaries in my life has been very difficult. Growing up, I did as I was told. I never questioned adults, and I always followed directions. This mind-set followed me into adulthood. I recall being told that a woman's place was in the house, so I set my mind that I was going to try to be the best at whatever I did and had become a perfectionist. I later learned that internal happiness was a choice and that I needed to focus on my well-being instead of pleasing others! How many of you know that you can become a pleaser to the point that you become a human doormat?

Unfortunately, it didn't matter how much of a pleaser I strove to be, nothing was ever good enough. I thought I had to be the perfect woman with a smile on my face all while I was being beaten down spiritually, physically, mentally, and emotionally. The pressure to be a pleaser was unbearable.

Learned behavior is difficult to change, but with God's help anything is possible. At one point in my life, it was difficult for me to say no to anyone, and as a result, I became dead inside. The more I gave, the more I felt that my efforts weren't enough.

Sadly, and to my detriment, the people around me continued

to take from me. It was as if I was wearing a magnet around my neck that attracted people who only wanted to take. Even though they claimed to care about me, no one gave, they took, and my tank was becoming emptier by the day, as there was no one there to replenish me. Most of my life was full of grief and disappoint.

I began to pray and ask God what was going on. To give me guidance as to how I should help myself, the Lord answered, "The problem is you."

I once read a quote: "You change for two reasons: either you learn enough that you want to, or you've been hurt enough that you have to" (Unknown).

Imagine what a sad, sad situation this is, finding yourself doing things, motivated out of feelings of guilt or obligation, and attempting to please others even at the expense of what's best for you. For some reason or another, you place your needs last, while you have allowed the needs of others to surpass your own.

My friends, I can honestly say this is one of the sadist devotionals I have written. Truthfully, to the people who fit this condition, I want you to know that this behavior doesn't serve either of the parties involved. We must find the courage to stand! If not, the end result will be the death of you.

If we say yes to others asking of our time and energy, while we've not yet satisfied our own needs first, we are giving from a position of lack. And when you give from a position of lack, you become resentful and bitter.

This is also a verdant breeding ground for codependent relationships. This will, in turn, make us attract people and situations that drain us because we aren't honoring our own needs and boundaries.

This abandonment of self generates anger and resentment, which, in turn, leaves us feeling powerless and causes contempt and distrust in our relationships.

The truth is, we're never victims of our circumstances. We can choose how we would like not only to perceive, but also to proceed to change our situation. It all starts with the mind! What is holding you back from honoring and loving yourself?

Remember: boundaries are important for your own growth and your well-being. Common fears that show up in the context of boundaries include fear of not being good enough, fear of rejection, and fear of being alone or abandoned. I was afraid of being alone and not being able to survive. I filled my head of the most ludicrous lies. I told myself that no one would love you and you would be left alone.

I lived in fear of my significant other leaving me because I was told this so many times that I began to believe that this will come to reality. I needed to prepare myself for this life event. So I chose to turn to the word of God. Reading self-help books, attending church on a regular basis, counseling, and studying the Bible. I began to gain strength and found peace within. I was finally okay to be alone. I knew that God would take care of me and my children.

Hebrews 4:12 (NIV) says, "For the word of God is alive and active. Sharper than any double-edged sword, it penetrates even to dividing soul and spirit, joints and marrow; it judges the thoughts and attitudes of the heart."

Biblically speaking, boundaries are related to self-control. The Bible commands us to control ourselves.

Titus 2:12 (NIV) says, "It teaches us to say 'No' to ungodliness and worldly passions, and to live self-controlled, upright and godly lives in this present age." it teaches us to value ourselves.

Boundaries are about taking responsibility for our own lives; we teach people how to treat us. The goal of establishing boundaries is to make sacrifices for people when appropriate, but never in a self-destructive way.

Ephesians 4:15 (NIV) explains, "Instead, speaking the truth in love, we will grow to become in every respect the mature body of him who is the head, that is, Christ."

In Romans 12:21 (NIV), God warns us, "Do not be overcome by evil, but overcome evil with good."

Love yourself enough to say no to what is not right. Do not allow yourself to be dragged so low to the point of no return. Read the word of God and allow it to transform your life. Tell yourself you are enough. Do not be afraid God is love. Then finally if someone wants to leave you, let them go! Your Redeemer lives! He is with you.

Are You in a Relationship That Requires You to Establish Boundaries?

_____

_____

_____

_____

_____

_____

_____

_____

_____

_____

_____

_____

How Do You Feel When You're Around Someone Who Takes You Out of Character?

_____

_____

_____

_____

_____

_____

List Ways You Can Change This

_____

_____

_____

_____

_____

_____

HEALTH TIP #32: **Dealing with Age Spots?**

"Age spots" or "liver spots" are flat, brown spots that can appear anywhere on the body as we age. These spots are the surface result of a waste build-up known as lipofuscin accumulation, a byproduct of free radical damage in skin cells. Age spots are usually due to liver toxicity or liver problems.

1. Liver Cleanse Formula, or Liv-J: this is a cleanse I have used. (Liver tonic/build/cleanse)
2. Milk Thistle T/R or Milk Thistle combination (rebuild liver)
3. Grapine High Potency (powerful antioxidant)
4. Vitamin C (this is an antioxidant and a vital nutrition for the body). You can buy vitamin C oil or vitamin C cream and apply to the skin, or buy vitamin Ctablets and take it internally.

One of my favorites is the Hepatic System Pack for the liver by Nature's Sunshine. Also mix fresh lemon juice and organic honey. Use as a facial mask daily. Leave for thirty minutes and splash with cold water.

DAY 33

WE ARE MIRRORS OF WHO IS IN FRONT OF US

Recently, a close friend and I were having a conversation about the reality and truth that we are, indeed, a "mirror of who is in front of us." Ever since this conversation, I've found myself secretly examining the nature of the people that are in my inner circle. I wonder, how am I like this person? What do we have in common?

In the humbleness of my being, I have learned that we are called not to judge others, so I try to live my life accordingly. In fact, when I counsel people, I often tell them that I love them regardless of whatever it is they have done. We live in a world where anything can happen at any time, and any one of us can fall into the pitfalls of life. It can be as simple as being in the wrong place at the wrong time. We all can attest to this in some shape or form.

This reminds me of a story about these two young brothers I knew. One of them, the oldest, ardently followed the rules and played it very safe; whereas, the other was the life of the party and took chances and risks.

The oldest of the two told me a story about a time they'd decided to go out partying together. In spite of their good intentions, they'd ended up spending the night in jail for drinking too much. The eldest, who was in college and aspired to receive his doctor's degree, had fallen asleep in the backseat of the car while the younger went to go find help to give their car a jump start. It just so happened that there was an on-duty police officer who came to their rescue. Realizing they were both under the influence, the officer decided to hold them overnight until they were sober again.

When I spoke to the oldest brother, I asked him what he had learned from his experience. In reply, he said, "I realized that no matter how good we try to be, it doesn't take much to mess up. It's important not to ever put yourself higher above anyone in life because you never know what can happen in any given day."

We live in a society where everyone is quick to pass judgment on one another, either with their words or actions. How about recognizing the greatness in everyone in spite of their circumstances?

Everyone you encounter is your mirror. What this means is that others reflect parts of your own consciousness back to you, giving you an opportunity to really see yourself and identify ways to grow and realize self-improvement. So many times we stand in a place of judgment and criticism of others not realizing that this may be coming from our own reflection of self.

Realize that the qualities you admire most in others are your own, and the same holds true for those qualities you dislike. The people whose personalities and actions tend to make us angry are generally the people we learn from the most. Those individuals serve as our mirrors and teach us what needs to be revealed about ourselves. Seeing what we don't like in others helps us to look deeper inside ourselves to change. Allow that view to exhilarate the need to begin healing, bring about balance, and change to improve yourself and become a better you.

A family member boasted on her children constantly and was quick to point out the wrongs others did. I did not like this one bit. She simply made me angry? How was I like her? I thought about this for quite a while and concluded we all have the potential of being judgmental. We don't want to accept these criticisms and would prefer to argue that we are not the arrogant, angry, violent, depressed, guilt-ridden, critical, or complaining person that we see in the mirror. The problems must not be mine, but lie with the other person, right?

A good question to ask yourself is, "If the problem truly is the other person's, why does being around this individual affect me so negatively?"

As life goes on and we face different challenges, I must encourage myself and urge my readers to constantly push yourself towards a higher connection with God. We will be confronted with situations, people, places, and so on that we find bothersome or uncomfortable to be around. However, it is in these circumstances that we are offered the greatest opportunity to learn more about ourselves.

As we learn what we need to do and adjust our lives accordingly, we will find that our mirrors will change. People will come and go from our lives, as we will always attract new mirror images for us to look at as we progress. For me, I will seek God and consciously strive to grow for the greater good. I will try to be an example of grace and excellence.

Hebrews 10:23–25 (NIV) says, "Let us hold unswervingly to the hope we profess, for He who promised is faithful. And let us consider how we may spur one another on toward love and good deeds, not giving up meeting together, as some are in the habit of doing, but encouraging one another—and all the more as you see the Day approaching."

In 1 Peter 4:8–10 (NIV), the Bible states, "Above all, love each other deeply, because love covers over a multitude of sins. Offer hospitality to one another without grumbling. Each of you should use whatever gift you have received to serve others, as faithful stewards of God's grace in its various forms."

Ephesians 4:29 (NIV) instructs, "Do not let any unwholesome talk come out of your mouths, but only what is helpful for building others up according to their needs, that it may benefit those who listen."

In 1 Thessalonians 5:14 (NIV), the Bible explains, "And we urge you, brothers and sisters, warn those who are idle and disruptive, encourage the disheartened, help the weak, be patient with everyone." Love one another as Christ loves the Church and never allow yourself to be in a place of superiority! We are all equal in the sight of God. Accept criticism and learn. Don't stand in a defensive, denying place, instead walk in humility as your father who created you did. Remember: I am you and you are me.

What Is Your Mirror's Reflection Trying to Teach You about Yourself?

_____

_____

_____

_____

_____

_____

_____

_____

_____

_____

_____

_____

HEALTH TIP #33: **Struggling with Anemia**

Anemia is when the blood lacks the right amount of healthy red blood cells. Causes of anemia may include recurring infections and disease, including low immunity, mineral deficiency, vitamin B12, folic acid deficiency, poor diet, poor food assimilation, candida autoimmune conditions, excessive menstruation, or alcoholism, and so on.

These are some of the herbs I have used and have gotten results from, they should be taken as directed Many of these can be found in tablet/capsule form.

1. Blood stimulator
2. Liquid B12 complete, which is necessary to properly assimilate iron
3. 1-X: an herbal iron formula
4. Dong quai—for high iron content
5. Super algae or spirulina—for iron
6. Milk thistle T/R helps rebuild the liver
7. Yellow dock, dandelion, mullein, or red raspberry
8. Zinc: Works with iron to build blood
9. Diet: Food high in organic iron. Examples: blackstrap molasses, dark green vegetables, red beets, and honey.

DAY 34

HE THAT HAS BEGUN A GOOD WORK IN YOU "SHALL" PERFORM IT UNTIL THE DAY OF JESUS CHRIST

Joshua 1:1–6 (NIV) says, "After the death of Moses, the servant of the Lord, the Lord said to Joshua son of Nun, Moses's aide: "Moses my servant is dead. Now then, you and all these people, get ready to cross the Jordan River into the land I am about to give to them—to the Israelites. I will give you every place where you set your foot, as I promised Moses. Your territory will extend from the desert to Lebanon, and from the great river, the Euphrates—all the Hittite country—to the Mediterranean Sea in the west. No one will be able to stand against you all the days of your life. As I was with Moses, so I will be with you; I will never leave you nor forsake you. Be strong and courageous, because you will lead these people to inherit the land I swore to their ancestors to give them."

Do not be afraid, for God is with you. Believe that He will bless you. There was a period of my life when God directed me to transition from owning a retail storefront to another path. At that time, I had owned a health food store, and having been there for eight years, I did not want to leave and had been holding onto it for dear life. The store had been struggling for the last couple years, and it was causing me stress and depression.

One day I walked into the store, and God told me to check the expiration dates on my products. Lo and behold, more than half of the products were expired and had to be pulled off the shelf. I had to shut the shop down!

The idea of transitioning from something that had been my focus and purpose was neither easy nor comfortable, but through this time, I heard the Lord repeatedly saying, "He that has begun a good work in you *shall* perform it until the day of Jesus Christ!"

I was fearful and worried, thinking about how I was going to pay my bills, where the help to empty the shop would come from, and all the other troubling aspects of this impending change. I allowed it to consume me.

Oh, but the God that we serve is a provider! He will provide a ram in the bush at the appropriate time. It came to me that I knew God had called me to preach, as I had completed my first book and was working on my second.

The day that I decided to close my doors for a few days to get my mind together happened to be on the same day that I was booked to minister at my first women's conference. That speaking engagement was very good for me and definitely a God ordained plan. My brothers and sisters, God has an answer for everything. God rained manna from heaven to bless his people, and we must trust God's answer even when we do not understand it.

In Exodus 16:4–5 (NIV), the Bible explains, "Then the

Lord said to Moses, "I will rain down bread from heaven for you. The people are to go out each day and gather enough for that day. In this way I will test them and see whether they will follow my instructions. On the sixth day they are to prepare what they bring in, and that is to be twice as much as they gather on the other days."

Believe that God will provide for us a supernatural blessing. Stand firm and believe that you will get what God has for you, which is always better than what you have for planned yourself. Get loose, get out of your comfort zone, and tell the devil that in Jesus's name you will receive what God has for you. Jeremiah 29:11–15 (NIV) says, "'For I know the plans I have for you,' declares the Lord, 'plans to prosper you and not to harm you, plans to give you hope and a future. Then you will call on me and come and pray to me, and I will listen to you. You will seek me and find me when you seek me with all your heart. I will be found by you,' declares the Lord, 'and will bring you back from captivity. I will gather you from all the nations and places where I have banished you,' declares the Lord, 'and will bring you back to the place from which I carried you into exile.'"

There is nothing the devil can throw at you that our sovereign God has not defeated. Nothing, absolutely nothing on this earth can keep God's promise from being fulfilled.

Hans Christian Andersen, a well-known Danish author, once said, "The life of a Christian is a series of miracles." I myself have experienced many miracles during my life, and I can attest to the fact that God will stop at nothing to save your life.

At one point in my life, I was contemplating suicide, and miraculously, two angels appeared to me and redirected my horrible thoughts. Thank God that He saved me, for this allowed me to spread the news of how much of a marvelous God we serve.

In my heart, I know that God has a "good work" that He will accomplish in my life and in yours. His purpose is for his children to conform into the image of Jesus Christ. He guards His children by His Spirit and with His Holy angels to ensure that none are lost during their earthly pilgrimage.

Jack Wyrtzen, a world-renowned Christian evangelist, loved to say, "I am as sure of heaven as if I'd already been there 10,000 years." How can we as Christians have the confidence to say that? Because it doesn't rest on me or you. It rests on the word of the eternal God. If God has said He is going to do it, He will! He is faithful indeed!

The question to ask ourselves is, do you believe that he has begun a good work in you?

Do You Recall a Time when God Gave You a Miracle?

_____

_____

_____

_____

_____

_____

_____

_____

_____

_____

HEALTH TIP #34: **Bites and Stings**

Bites and stings from different bugs and animals have the possibility to be very dangerous to our health. The animal or bug can carry different bacteria and germs, or even venom which can have negative effects, especially on the young, old, or those with compromised immune systems. Seek appropriate medical assistance for serious bites and stings as well as allergic reactions:

Topical/External Treatment
- Use activated charcoal—mix with water and (oil) and apply to neutralize the poison. For multiple stings, open several capsules of charcoal into tub. Add warm water and immerse the body.
- Black cohosh—use as a poultice is effective for bites and stings.

Internal (to be taken as directed; can usually be found in capsule or liquid form)
- Black cohosh
- MSM—to bind foreign proteins such as insects and snake bites
- Nature's Immune Stimulator
- Pantothenic Acid (for unexplained itching)

Essential Oils That May Alleviate the Effects
- Patchouli (antidote for snake and insect bites)
- Peppermint—to repel bugs

DAY 35

GOD WILL SILENCE THE SLANDEROUS ACCUSERS OF THE BRETHREN

The slanderous accuser standeth here and slumbereth not! He is the accuser who comes to destroy!

As I sit here in silence, composing my thoughts for this day, my soul is saddened for the ones who will easily fall into the traps of the accuser. I believe God wants to send you a direct message today: The devil will use those close to you to tell lies about you, and he will try to reverse the good that you do. Whatever the case may be, God has sent me to tell you to continue to stand strong in Him.

Jesus himself was wrongfully accused, yet He offered no defense against the baseless charges. Imagine how He must have felt when He was accused? Condemned to death? Beaten, humiliated, and put through public humiliation? Yet He rose again!

Even as our Savior Jesus Christ was slandered and hurt by those whom He helped and loved, surely there is a chance we will also encounter this in our own lives. In Revelations 12:7–12 (NIV), the Bible reports, "Then war broke out in heaven. Michael and his angels fought against the dragon, and the dragon and his angels fought back. But he was not strong enough, and they lost their place in heaven. The great dragon was hurled down—that ancient serpent called the devil, or Satan, who leads the whole world astray. He was hurled to the earth, and his angels with him. Then I heard a loud voice in heaven say: 'Now have come the salvation and the power and the kingdom of our God, and the authority of his Messiah. For the accuser of our brothers and sisters, who accuses them before our God day and night, has been hurled down. They triumphed over him by the blood of the Lamb and by the word of their testimony; they did not love their lives so much as to shrink from death. Therefore rejoice, you heavens and you who dwell in them! But woe to the earth and the sea, because the devil has gone down to you! He is filled with fury, because he knows that his time is short.'"

The devil has been a murderer and a conniver from the beginning of time, and his goal is to see us fall, but the good news is that God has power over darkness.

In 1 John 3:8 (NIV), the Bible explaions, "The one who does what is sinful is of the devil, because the devil has been sinning from the beginning. The reason the Son of God appeared was to destroy the devil's work."

In Colossians 2:15 (NIV), the Bible also says, "And having disarmed the powers and authorities, He made a public spectacle of them, triumphing over them by the cross."

It's important for us as believers to know that we are also susceptible to falling into situation of being slandered by our brothers and sisters. God warns us not to circulate a false report. In Exodus 23:1 (NIV), the scripture instructs, "Do not spread false reports. Do not help a guilty person by being a malicious witness."

Many can't resist the temptation to gossip, especially when slander and lies are involved. Slander, which means "to defame someone; to harm their reputation; to disgrace; or to accuse," is a way to cause hatred and division among us. We must stand firm and believe that God will defend us.

In 1 Peter 3:15–16 (NIV), God says, "But do this with gentleness and respect, keeping a clear conscience, so that those who speak maliciously against your good behavior in Christ may be ashamed of their slander."

Satan is a liar, and he is the father of deception. The first time Satan appears in the Bible, in Genesis 3:1 (NIV), the first words on his lips were to question the truth. "Did God say you shall not eat any tree in the garden?"

He blinds the minds of unbelievers and has ways of turning them against others. In this verse I caution you to take notice of the first thing Satan did. He questioned the truth! When the same situation arises in your life, realize who it is and get into your war room.

The devil speaks falsely and hides and disguises the truth. When he lies, he speaks according to his own nature. He is the father of lies. Jesus said to those who were planning to kill him, "You belong to your father, the devil, and you want to carry out your father's desires. He was a murderer from the beginning, not holding to the truth, for there is no truth in him. When he lies, he speaks his native language, for he is a liar and the father of lies" (John 8:44 NIV).

My brothers and sisters, how we respond to mistreatment is one of the most important aspects of your spiritual life. We must not allow the bitterness of slanderous words to overtake our hearts, as hurt and unforgiveness will defile our spirits and dull our ability to sense the presence of God or hear his voice. Give your accusers into God's hands and trust and follow Jesus.

In the same vein, do no harm against those around you; cast out all negative thoughts and lies against your brothers and sisters. Don't become a pawn for the devil by spreading false allegations and slanderous words, as not only could it easily be done unto you, but also it hurts our Father in heaven to see us tear each other down instead of lifting each other up.

Who shall lay anything to the charge of God's elect? He is the king of glory, and He knows His children. There are no accusers that we have to be afraid of before God. We need not fear damnation, knowing that we rest upon the death and resurrection, the almighty power and defense of Jesus Christ. Free yourself from being a constant critic and fault finder. Remember that the Bible doesn't promise peace to those who dwell on the faults and blame of others!

In Isaiah 26:3 (NIV), we are told, "You will keep in perfect peace those whose minds are steadfast, because they trust in you."

Be still and watch God silence your accusers! Thank Him, victory belongs to you. Our God is the light of this world. We belong to Jesus!

Are You an Accuser of Your Brethren?

_____

_____

_____

_____

_____

_____

Allow God to Heal Your Heart from Your Own Pain, Hurt, and Unforgiveness.

_____

_____

_____

_____

_____

_____

HEALTH TIP #35: **Bladder Infection**

A bladder infection is an inflammation of the wall and lining of the urinary bladder. Symptoms include frequent urination, cloudy or bloody urine, with pain and tenderness in the lower abdomen. Causes of the infection may include hormonal changes, antibiotics, stress, antibacterial soaps, sprays, douches, feminine deodorants, contraceptive jellies and creams, and so on.

Primary Formulas (to be taken as directed; can be found in capsule or liquid form)

- Cranberry Buchu or Urinary Maintenance
- Urinary System Pack
- KB-C (Chinese kidney/bone)
- Juniper berries
- Lobelia—reduces bladder spasms
- Cornsilk, hydrangea, or parsley (natural diuretic)—reduces inflammation
- MSM—for pain and inflammation
- Probiotic—helps increase friendly bacteria

Drinking cranberry juice without sugar has also been known to help with bladder infections.

DAY 36

LOOK TO THE HILLS FROM WHENCE YOUR HELP COMETH FROM

In my life, I have failed, been hurt by the ones I trusted, and fallen short of being my best self. It was when I surrendered my all to Jesus and trusted Him to carry me through life, then I was able to rest and find peace. God has always been able to handle all my problems and strife better than I could have ever imagined doing it by myself. Therefore, put your troubles in his hands. In Psalm 21:5–7 (NIV), the psalmist writes, "Through the victories you have gotten, His glory is great; you have bestowed on Him splendor and majesty. Surely you have granted Him unending blessings and made Him glad with the joy of your presence. For the king trusts in the Lord; through the unfailing love of the Most High, he will not be shaken." This is the powerful word of God.

"Be still before the Lord and wait patiently for Him; do not fret when people succeed in their ways, when they carry out their wicked schemes" (Psalm 37:7 NIV).

Deliberately shut the door on all negative surroundings and clatter to focus on God and God alone. Seek the Lord and find His secret place—a place where you can commune and be with Him. Only in silence will you hear him. Stay in the secret hiding place of the most high God and allow Him to protect you. In His hiding place, you will find refuge and peace that super exceeded all understanding. By doing this, you are dying to the flesh and surrendering your all into God's hands.

Dying to the fleshly desires happens when we wait upon the Lord and place seeking Him as our utmost importance. Stay in the presence of the Lord and allow Him to transform you. They that wait upon the Lord receive strength. When you are in the presence of God, something happens that is beautiful and miraculous. In Psalm 40:1–2 (NIV), the Bibles says, "I waited patiently for the Lord; He turned to me and heard my cry. He lifted me out of the slimy pit, out of the mud and mire; He set my feet on a rock and gave me a firm place to stand."

Allow Jesus to become more real to you than your earthly desires, your thoughts, and whatever pains you find yourself going through. When He becomes real to you, you will find comfort and will relax, knowing that your God will handle even the worst of your situations. You are able to understand that even in the midst of all your travails He is working on your behalf and that the final victory will always be yours. If you feel broken and full of grief, if you feel as if you have lost everything, faint not! Our God is the God of new beginnings! There is no door that He cannot open. Look to the hills from whence your help cometh.

Softly and tenderly, Jesus is calling, "Come home, ye who are weary, come home." (Randy Travis. Softly and Tenderly) You need only to heed His call. Our enemy is lousy, he wants to destroy us by polluting our minds with lies and hatred. But we must not fear because Jesus came to give us life.

My friends, today I urge you to stoke a burning desire for our Savior, Jesus Christ. Repent with an honest heart and a hungering need for our Savior. Remember that He knows your heart. Go to Him with sincerity and true repentance, and He will forgive you for your sins because He understands our daily struggles. Praise Him with your whole heart.

When the glory of God comes upon you, it is the most beautiful experience of all! The Lord will speak through you, heal through you, and use you as His vessel to minister the gospel. In His presence, there is great peace. But, if you want to be exalted in the Holy Ghost, be meek in the spirit. God does not want a show-off or someone who turns down their nose at their brothers and sisters, for we are all made equal. Remember: it is not your ability; it is His ability working through you. Life in the spirit with sincerity and love is the only life God will accept.

God will make His way clear to you—ask Him for the path, and He will show you where He is. Surrender completely. Surrender to Him, give Him not only your heart, love, and body, but also your pain, suffering, and troubles. God is looking for people He can trust.

Do not miss the opportunity to accept Him as your Savior. Do not allow yourselves to suffer any longer. Surrender all to Him and walk with Jesus in your journey here on earth until glory—He is always with you.

Do You Believe You Have Died to Your Flesh?

List habits that could be hindering your walk.

_____

_____

_____

_____

_____

_____

_____

_____

_____

_____

_____

_____

HEALTH TIP #36: **Cold Sores**

Cold sores appear as a small blister on the lips and face and are caused by the herpes virus.

Herbals
- Olive leaf extract (antiviral)
- Echinacea/ Goldenseal (immune stimulant/ antiviral)
- Elderberry (antiviral to build immune system)
- Black walnut (antiparasitic)

Vitamins/Minerals
- L-lysine (antiviral amino acid)
- Vitamin C and zinc
- Colostrum (improve immune response to viruses)
- Silver Shield (antiviral) can be used internally and externally

Replace your toothbrush after the blister has formed and again after attack is over. Silver Shield gel used externally will remove sores quickly.

DAY 37

WE MAY NOT BE PERFECT, BUT JESUS THOUGHT WE WERE TO DIE FOR

Before I began writing this chapter, I wanted to hear a good word that would lift my spirits. I searched through the words of several well-known pastors that would give a good old Pentecostal preaching before finally settling on a preacher who I resonated with. As I listened, though, I felt great sadness come over me because he began to make fun of himself simply because he was overweight. The crowd laughed while he jeered and made a few more jokes at his own expense, going on, and making light of his clothing and how his jeans that could not button all the way up. My brother went on.

Don't get me wrong: I am by no means criticizing my dear brother in Christ; however, this triggered painful memories of my own. You see, I myself have also been guilty of overly criticizing myself. There was a point in my life where I thought I was too fat, my nose wasn't pointed, or I was too short. You know, the critical things we all think of ourselves?

What made this even worse was that I also had outside forces putting me through the wringer, which, in turn, made me criticize myself even further. I was in a terrible state of self-sabotage. I have encountered people who had tried to destroy me at every turn, but our God is a mighty God! He delivered me from the lion's den of my attackers. Today, instead of criticizing something about myself, I ask God to help me to change my mind and see myself through His eyes. Jesus wants us to accept who we are, imperfections and all.

Most of us spend time criticizing our looks, which inhibits our ability to move forward. We tell ourselves what we cannot do instead of reminding ourselves of what God can do through us. Self-hate and negative thoughts about ourselves puts us on a dangerous path where we fail to see the greatness that God has placed in us, hindering our growth.

You must learn and know that the Lord loves you and that you are made perfect in His eyes. Today the Lord wants me to tell you that even though you may not be perfect in the narrow scope of the world, He still thinks you're to die for. In Psalm 139:14 (NIV), the Bible says, "I praise you because I am fearfully and wonderfully made; your works are wonderful, I know that full well."

My friends, the truth is you are the carefully designed creation of a great and loving God. You may not "look perfect," "act perfect," or achieve everything you set out to do, but that doesn't change how He feels about you. You are truly beautiful in His sight.

Honor the Lord by honoring yourself. He believes in you, all you need to do is place your hands in His and trust Him to change all the self-hate and self-criticism that you might be struggling with.

Having a healthy self-esteem, loving and accepting yourself for who you are, is important because not only does life become simpler but also you lessen the opportunities for self-sabotage. This allows you to make decisions that can better your life and helps you to find stability in a world of negativity and uncertainty.

I love the quote by M. Scott Peck, a well-known psychiatrist and author: "Until you value yourself, you won't value your time. Until you value your time, you will not do anything with it."

Another good quote that comes to mind is from everyone's favorite neighbor, Fred Rogers: "If you could only sense how important you are to the lives of those you meet; how important you can be to the people you may never even dream of. There is something of yourself that you leave at every meeting with another person."

When you adopt the viewpoint that there is nothing that exists that is not part of you, you will value and see yourself the way God sees you. I pray that you reach for the Lord Jesus Christ and ask Him to help you to begin to love yourself. You must take the chance to risk being seen in all of your glory; God has called you for something greater than yourself.

Are You Self-Sabotaging by Criticizing Yourself?

_____

_____

_____

_____

_____

_____

Write Ways That You Can Begin to Make Changes:

_____

_____

_____

_____

_____

_____

_____

HEALTH TIP #37: **Gallbladder Issues**

The gallbladder is a small, pear-shaped muscular sac located under the right lobe of the liver into which bile secreted by the liver is stored until needed by the body for digestion. In my opinion, having this organ removed will not serve you. It's better to take care of your body. Symptoms of gallbladder problems usually include pain under the right ribcage or between shoulder blades, nausea after eating, or chalk-colored stools.

Primary Formula
Gallbladder formula (liver tonic/ aid digestion)

Herbs
- Blood stimulator—use at least six months to strengthen gallbladder before any gallbladder cleanse.

Vitamins, Minerals, and Other Supplements
- Digestive Bitters Tonic—aids cleansing of gall bladder and digest fats properly
- Hi Lipase—enzyme to digest fats
- Bowel detox—contains bile salts for digestion. Essential if there has been gallbladder surgery.
- Thai-Go, vitamin A, vitamin C

Gallstones
- Hydrangea—to pass gallstones
- Cascara sagrada—increase bile flow to dissolve gallstones

- Digestive bitters tonic—helps the gallbladder empty
- Liver cleanse formula—to pass gallstones

Pain: Castor oil pack on liver/gallbladder area

Diet: Apple juice, apple sauce, and figs. Pears, pear juice, beet juice. Avoid all fats. Grate one tablespoon raw beet in salad each day. It's your heavenly Father's desire that you have good health. Honor Him by honoring the gift He has given you—your body!

DAY 38

DON'T GIVE UP BEFORE YOUR BREAKTHROUGH— YOUR REDEEMER LIVES

I remember when I was a little girl in my home of Guyana, our country was in a time of upheaval and riots, and the authorities would not allow people to leave their homes. In spite of the dangers that lurked outside, my mother braved the storms, took a chance, and went to work anyway. She was willing to risk death by torture to feed her ten children and provide for her family.

When it came to fears about being hurt, or worse, killed, I can recall her saying, "It's appointed unto a man to die once." My mother also had a great belief in God and often said, "If God provides for the bird in the air; surely, he will provide for me and my children." Her fearlessness and trust in the Lord continue to inspire me to go on even through the hardest of times. You see, Satan will try to instill fear into you but God is calling us to be brave.

Before the completion of this book, the devil came at me hard several times, and at one point I wondered, "Where is God in all of this?" There were times I felt despair, as if my enemies had triumphed over me, as if I had lost. But of course, I was in my feelings, unable to see through the fear and turmoil of my troubles. As I reflected in my quiet time, I was able to see that God had control of the entire situation and that He was embracing me and carrying me along. As my mother did for her children, God always provided for me and my needs.

The devil thought he had ensnared me hook, line, and sinker! But God! You see, my friends, evil cannot triumph over good! The truth is the truth; that being the victory is always ours, and God will set you free—free indeed!

This brings me to my question: What are you asking God to do for you? It is important to ask yourself this because you must get clear on exactly what it is that you want. This also helps make your breakthrough feel more tangible and closer to the unfolding of God's purpose.

Go to the Lord with confidence and clarity and see the miracles that He places before you—see that He is always behind the scenes to turn the situation in your favor. Don't give up before you attain your breakthrough, your Redeemer lives! Remember, my brothers and sisters: the greater the challenge, the bigger your victory!

Deuteronomy 20:4 (NIV) explains, "For the Lord your God is the one who goes with you to fight for you against your enemies to give you victory." He further states in 1 Corinthians 10:13 (NIV), "No temptation has overtaken you except what is common to mankind. And God is faithful; He will not let you be tempted beyond what you can bear. But when you are tempted, He will also provide a way out so that you can endure it." In reading this verse, it gives me comfort knowing that nothing happens unless God allows it to come to pass.

The Bible tells us to keep our eyes fixed on Jesus, the author and finisher of our faith. Oftentimes, right before your victory, difficulties may come against you; but you have got to keep looking forward into the eyes of Jesus. When you feel as though you are about to fall, it might actually be that you are about to fly. No matter what your situation looks like, refuse to quit, as your blessings are right around the corner and God will scatter your enemy like the dust before the winds. Keep trying, keep fighting, keep hoping, and most importantly, keep believing in your Father.

Holy Spirit, I welcome you in every aspect of my life. Be my protector, comfort me and guide me through this present state of turmoil. Help me not to feel like a failure but give me the strength to face what is to come. Help me and comfort me in knowing that failure is the doorway to having great success. Father, give me hope as I cling to you in Jesus's name.

Do You Feel as If You Are on the Verge of Giving Up?

Cite Scriptures of Encouragement and Believe
God Will Come Through for You.

_____

_____

_____

_____

_____

_____

_____

_____

_____

_____

HEALTH TIP #38: **Bad Breath**

Bad breath (halitosis) is usually caused from poor dental hygiene, dehydration, or underlying illnesses such as liver problems, kidney problems, or issues in the lower digestive tract. It can also be caused by infection in the gums to name a few.

Herbs (taken as directed)
- Liquid chlorophyll—to cleanse the body and as a natural deodorizer
- Liquid cleanse, colon cleanse
- Small intestine detox—remove mucus from small intestine
- Enviro—detox or all cell detox
- Liver Balance—for metallic breath caused by a stressed liver
- Essential oil—peppermint

DAY 39

GIANTS DO FALL

We all know the very familiar story of David and Goliath: David, a young shepherd boy, boldly defeated the giant Goliath, armed only with a slingshot and five smooth stones. The terror of the Philistines was eliminated, and the Israelites were reinvigorated because a little shepherd boy answered the call of God and stood in battle with the undefeatable giant. A boy who had no fear.

The Bible tells us, "As the Philistine moved closer to attack him, David ran quickly toward the battle line to meet him" (1 Samuel 17:48 NIV). The scripture tells us that as the enemy drew closer, David ran to confront him. My question to you, do you run closer or you run away from your giants?

Whatever giant or giants you might be facing, the time has come to face them. Stop rationalizing the situation, stop excusing it, and realize that you cannot defeat it by your strength alone.

This brings me to a happening that occurred a few nights ago. For some reason unbeknownst to me, the Lord would not allow me to sleep. I had this insatiable need to just pray. I resorted to laying across the living room floor, on my belly. I wept, I prayed, and I cried out aloud for all to hear me.

I prayed for everyone around me; when suddenly, I began

to pray for and focus on my second son. At one point, I just kept calling out his name and specifically asked the Lord to send seventy-two thousand angels to encamp around him and to protect him.

The next day my son called me and said, "Mom, Jesus is real!" When I asked him what happened, he told me that he and some friends had been out partying when a fight had broken out. His friends had run off and abandoned him as three men came after him to beat him. My son told me that one of them punched him, but it hadn't hurt, and that all of a sudden, the very person who'd punched him had begun to scream—jumping up and down as if someone was pistol-whipping him. The other two watched with their eyes popping out in wonder before all three men took off running!

To God be the glory! My beloved friends, trust in the Lord. Don't look at your giant with the eyes of defeat; instead, look at it in the light of God's amazing power to fight on your behalf!

Who or what is your giant? Are you facing some form of addiction? Could it be that you are overly critical of yourself? Your finances are sinking and you can't seem to catch yourself as your debt mounts? Are you lonely and feel as if no one cares? Do you feel as if your looming giant is bigger than you, stronger than you, faster than you, and heavier than you are able to carry?

My friends, believe that God will crush the jaws of your giants. I don't know what God has done for you in your life, but I am sure that if you look, you will find that He has saved you numerous times. Don't give up hope! God cares.

In 1 Peter 5:9 (NIV), the Bible instructs us, "Resist him,

standing firm in the faith, because you know that the family of believers throughout the world is undergoing the same kind of sufferings."

God wants you to win. He wants you to grow and overcome. He wants you to testify of his goodness.

In 2 Corinthians 10:4–5 (NIV), we are told, "The weapons we fight with are not the weapons of the world. On the contrary, they have divine power to demolish strongholds. We demolish arguments and every pretension that sets itself up against the knowledge of God, and we take captive every thought to make it obedient to Christ."

In 2 Corinthians 6:18 (NIV), the Bible says, "And, I will be a Father to you, and you will be my sons and daughters, says the Lord Almighty."

In your journey of life, you are going to face giants; you are going to have to stand against enemies far too powerful for you to handle on your own. But, my friends, remember: in all this, you are never alone.

Remember: in your toughest battles, in the midst of fights where you find yourself over your head, you can believe that He will make you into a giant slayer for He has come to set the captive free.

In 1 Chronicles 16:11–22 (NIV), the Bible commands, "Look to the Lord and His strength; seek His face always. Remember the wonders He has done, His miracles, and the judgments He pronounced, you His servants, the descendants of Israel, His chosen ones, the children of Jacob. He is the Lord our God; His judgments are in all the earth. He remembers His covenant forever, the promise He made, for a thousand generations, the covenant He made with Abraham, the oath He swore to Isaac. He confirmed it to Jacob as a decree, to Israel as an everlasting covenant: 'To you I will give the land of Canaan as the portion you will inherit.' When they were but few in number, few indeed, and strangers in it, they wandered from nation to nation, from one kingdom to another. He allowed no one to oppress them; for their sake He rebuked kings: 'Do not touch my anointed ones; do my prophets no harm.'"

What Is the Giant That You Are Asking God to Smite?

_____

_____

_____

_____

_____

_____

_____

_____

_____

_____

_____

HEALTH TIP #39: **Want to Flush Pounds of Toxins from Your Body?**

Toxins in the body can be picked up from the foods we eat, pollution, pesticides, medication and more. The effects can be shown by way of constant fatigue, stubborn weight gain, aches and pains, and skin reactions. I have come across a mixture that will helps rid the body of toxins, cleanse the colon, and remove inches from your waist. Drink this every morning before breakfast.

1. 1 organic lemon, not peeled
2. 1 piece of ginger, not peeled
3. 1 teaspoon of sea salt
4. 1 organic apple
5. 1 cup of purified water

Add the ingredients to a blender, blend thoroughly, and enjoy. This mixture has worked for me in the past, and it's one that I've continually used on a recurring basis. I recommend the use of this for up to six weeks for optimal results. This natural drink will improve your quality of health, and it will increase your energy.

DAY 40

I BELIEVE IN SIGNS, MIRACLES, AND THE HEALING POWER OF JESUS CHRIST

In Mark 16:17–20 (NIV), Jesus said, "And these signs will accompany those who believe: In my name they will drive out demons; they will speak in new tongues; they will pick up snakes with their hands; and when they drink deadly poison, it will not hurt them at all; they will place their hands on sick people, and they will get well." After the Lord Jesus had spoken to them, he was taken up into heaven and he sat at the right hand of God. Then the disciples went out and preached everywhere, and the Lord worked with them and confirmed his word by the signs that accompanied it."

To me, this is absolutely incredible! When I ponder upon these words, I come to the realization that our sole purpose here on this earth is to do God's will, follow His teachings, believe and trust in Him with our entire heart and soul, and allow Him to do great things through us. We are living to live again and our destination of heaven is the most amazing, peaceful, and beautiful place; there are no worries, anguish, or pain there. To me it's a win-win deal: follow Jesus, witness a most amazing life, and when it's all over, experience a heavenly place.

Before I started writing this book, I was given a vision of heaven, a vision of the most beautiful place where all kinds of flowers and plants bloomed. Flowers of all vibrant shades and colors, that my eyes had never seen before, surrounded me, with fragrance that enveloped me.

The peace I felt in this place was indescribable. People were dressed all in white and walked far off in the distance; my presence unbeknownst to them. I stood and watch them from a distance. They had so much joy. It was simply divine!

As I admired my surroundings and basked in the tranquility, Jesus appeared in front of me. I stood in front of my Father and felt the most amazing sense of love I have ever experienced wash over me. His presence was powerful and all encompassing! There was a tremendous divine light radiating off of Him; however, I could make out a silhouette of His face. I knew instantly that I belong there with Him. I was free, in total peace and at home!

As I stood in front of Him, I felt that I did not want to ever leave; that I wanted to stay and bask in His love. But I heard Him say ever so gently that I must return and that my time on earth was not finished. He told me there were still unfinished things left for me to accomplish.

Standing in front of Jesus, I can recall saying again that I did not want to leave, when all of a sudden, I felt an energy pulling me from Him. In desperation, I looked up to Jesus and, grabbing onto his hand, asked Him, "Will I see you again?"

Lovingly, He nodded yes, and my beautiful vision ended. My beloved, I can tell you that there is no competition between here on earth and our reward in heaven. Compared to heaven, earth is a massive graveyard, a dead place. This vision is what inspired the title of this book, *I Placed My Hands in His*.

God wants us to know that this life is only a temporary journey and our final and permanent destination is heaven. I have gone through trials and tribulations, and felt as though I did not belong here on earth. But while standing in front of Jesus, I knew without a shadow of a doubt where and to whom I belonged!

Wherever you are, whomever you are, whatever you are doing—stop and give God a praise, glorify His name, and worship Him. He is indeed a wonder! Accept him as your Savior; repent of your sins.

In Matthew 10:7–8 (NIV), the Bible says, "As you go, proclaim this message: 'The kingdom of heaven has come near.' Heal the sick, raise the dead, cleanse those who have leprosy, drive out demons. Freely you have received; freely give."

My beloved friends, the time is here and now. We must understand that we are all here for a single divine purpose. Will you choose this day to allow God to lead you into His will for your life? The day will come when you too will have the opportunity to stand directly in front of Him. Picture that for a moment, and He will say to you, "Well done, my good and faithful servant."

Our God is a miracle-working God, a healer, a mender, and a fixer. Throughout my life, I have experienced numerous miracles, but the one that stands out in my mind was my very first experience of amazement of the Lord.

I knew in that moment that there was a greater power than myself. I can remember being about seven or eight years old and playing with some of my friends by the riverside. Our plans that day were to dig into the mud holes that littered the sides of the water and find where the baby crabs were hiding.

As we played (as young children do), I had this great idea to go for a swim. Since I was the leader of my young friends, and knowing how dangerous the water was, I instructed them to watch from the sides.

Unfortunately, I couldn't swim, and to make matters worse, the canal had just been opened, unleashing a rushing current of water that began to pull me deeper and deeper into the river. I struggled to scream for help as all my little friends ran off. I just knew I was finished.

As the current of the water took me further out, I could feel my body growing limp. I was drowning! All of a sudden, I felt a firm hand grab me, and the next thing I remember is finding myself on shore. It all happened so quickly. Despite there being no one in sight, I knew that someone had saved my life.

In fear, I got up and ran home as fast as my legs would carry me. When my friends saw me alive and well, they stared at me with their eyes popped open as if they had seen a ghost. Imagine my shock when they told me that they hadn't gone for help, despite seeing me in danger, for fear of being in trouble themselves.

Sadly, and I didn't know it at the time, this was my first encounter with abandonment, which, in turn, was the beginning of my trust issues that plagued me through much of my life. Nevertheless, looking back, I realize that God saved me because it was not my time to die.

I tell this story to reaffirm that only God knows the plan

He has for us. So many of us live our lives in fear. Fear of death, fear of sickness, fear of not being able to be productive or, in my case, fear of failure.

My dear friends, it is impossible to fail with Jesus as your Lord and Savior.

I once read a quote that stands out in my mind, "Fear has two meanings—Forget Everything and Run, or Face Everything and Rise."

The choice is yours! Believe that God can do a miracle for you.

Have you ever experienced something supernatural that could not be resolved in humanly circumstances? If you have, then you too have experienced a miracle as evidence that Jesus lives!

Jesus is also a healer.

This brings me to the question I was always curious about. What is the purpose of miraculous gifts? As I pondered upon this question, it became obvious that the purpose in performing miracles was to establish His credentials and identify Him as the Messiah, the son of God.

I needed to make this clear in my writings because not everyone will experience healing in the same way. In spite of our circumstances, we must trust our Savior, knowing and understanding that He always knows best.

In John 16:12–14 (NIV), Jesus said, "I have much more to say to you, more than you can now bear. But when He, the Spirit of truth, comes, he will guide you into all the truth. He will not speak on his own; He will speak only what He hears, and He will tell you what is yet to come. He will glorify me because it is from Me that he will receive what He will make known to you."

In Matthew 5:17–20 (NIV), Jesus also said, "Do not think that I have come to abolish the Law or the Prophets; I have not come to abolish them but to fulfill them. For truly I tell you, until heaven and earth disappear, not the smallest letter, not the least stroke of a pen, will by any means disappear from the Law until everything is accomplished. Therefore, anyone who sets aside one of the least of these commands and teaches others accordingly will be called least in the kingdom of heaven, but whoever practices and teaches these commands will be called great in the kingdom of heaven. For I tell you that unless your righteousness surpasses that of the Pharisees and the teachers of the law, you will certainly not enter the kingdom of heaven."

In John 14:2–4 (NIV), Jesus also said, "My Father's house has many rooms; if that were not so, would I have told you that I am going there to prepare a place for you? And if I go and prepare a place for you, I will come back and take you to be with me that you also may be where I am. You know the way to the place where I am going."

As I bring this book to a conclusion, I want to reiterate that I did promise to be transparent with you all.

So from my heart to yours, my beloved, I have lived on this Earth for fifty years and most of it has been filled with disappointments, trials, hurdles, tribulations, pain, and sorrow, but I will never change a thing! I have seen God do great things in my life.

This life is not our final destination. Be encouraged today and reach out and place your hands in His—walk with Him. There is a place in Glory with your name on it!

My Sisters and Brothers, Are You Living Now to Live Again Later in Glory with Jesus?

Do You Want to Fulfill the Purpose God Has for You Here on Earth?

_____

_____

_____

_____

_____

_____

_____

_____

_____

_____

HEALTH TIP #40: Use Nutmeg, Cinnamon, Honey, and Lemon Juice to Benefit the Skin

Your skin is your largest organ and a barrier against infection, so it's very important to take care of it. Nutmeg has great beauty benefits. It is packed with antibacterial, antiseptic, analgesic, anti-inflammatory, and antioxidant properties. It provides numerous beauty benefits, such as eliminating acne, eczema, and preventing aging. Nutmeg oils are often found in facial cleansers and moisturizers. It cleans the skin, promotes circulation, and fights free radicals.

- Cinnamon is rich in antifungal and antiviral properties. Prevents premature aging.
- Honey: Promotes healing and detoxifying for the skin. Promotes healing.
- Lemon: Helps build collagen in skin, keeps skin young and firm. It reduces pores and lightens dark spots.

Mix a small amount of each together and apply two to three times weekly, wait till dry, and splash rinse with cold water. Once done, gently pat dry. Be good to yourselves, and I pray that you continue to seek natural ways in honoring your body. In return you will enjoy a full life. God bless you all.

Dear readers,

It is an honor and a blessing to have the opportunity to connect with you. I am humbled and grateful that you would take the time to read the messages God has inspired in me. We are all striving for better each day.

And I thank you! I am interested in you and your story. I am your sister in Christ. My contact information will be in the back of this book. I have also gotten a P. O. Box address so that you can write to me. I would love to hear from you. I pray the blessings of God upon your life. I love you all in Jesus's name.

—Selene

PRAYER FOR SALVATION

We have all been created for greater things. In His image, we do His work. Each life is precious to God. He created the world in His magnificence and created mankind to share His creation. We only have to look for His goodness everywhere, and accept His concern for us. When we turn our life over to Him and live according to His will, we will know that He will direct our paths for His purpose. Yoked to Him, our burden is light and easy. God wants us to communicate with Him in every moment and bring any care or concern to Him. All loneliness, despair or hopelessness ceases in His enveloping love for each of us.

REPEAT THIS PRAYER

Precious Jesus, I come to you a broken vessel. I ask you to forgive me of my sins and set me free from the works of my enemies and from the traps of Satan. Lead me from despair to renewed hope. Come into my life and change me. I accept you as my savior, Jesus Christ, who died for my sins. I thank you for removing fear from my mind and helping me to trust again. Fill me with your love, so that I can forgive. Allow me to feel your presence and your peace. Change my will, desires, and wants, and let it line up with yours, in Jesus's name. Amen.

> For it is with your heart that you believe and
> are justified, and it is with your mouth that
> you profess your faith and are saved.
> —Romans 10:10 (NIV)

ABOUT THE AUTHOR

Dr. Selene M. Author, DNM, MH, CNHP, is a member of the American Naturopathic Medical Certification Board, and a board-certified doctor of natural medicine, nutritionist, and master herbalist with over twenty-five years of experience using natural herbs and remedies. In addition, Selene is a motivational speaker, life coach, educator, philanthropist, advocate of various social causes, and founder of Silent Cry Loud Echo Ministries. She is a graduate of Trinity College of Natural Health and the Institute of the National Association of Certified Natural Professionals. Dr. Author has her own private practice, Nature's Way to Health, where the motto is, "Thought is Perception."

Selene was the youngest of ten children on the northeastern side of South America in the country of Guyana. The family lived off the land, learning the basics of survival to stay healthy and mentally cognitive, with the ability to heal from common illnesses. Young Selene developed a passion for true healing during her adolescent years and became committed to finding answers for not only herself and her family, but for society at large. She is an inspirational mentor, motivational speaker, and evangelist who teaches others to free and love themselves with mental, emotional, physical, and spiritual guidance.

Selene has a passion for mission work, having placed ten

wells in South America thus far. One of her passions is to speak to the nations regarding domestic violence, child abuse, and the devastating effects they cause everyone involved. Dr. Author is passionate about changing lives.

When Selene is not public speaking, teaching, or traveling, she sees individuals for one on one appointments in her private practice. Using holistic therapies, homeopathic remedies, and herbal medicines in combination with nutritional and lifestyle counseling, Selene addresses the full dynamic of individual health care.

"Because of the genius of our Creator, through Jesus Christ, the body has the ability to heal itself!" she says. Selene is a stalwart voice of faith and inspiration.

She can be reached at

P.O. Box 2369, Prince Frederick, MD 20678

doctork4625@gmail.com